IT ALL STARTS WITH
YOU

The Power of
Pre-Emptive Leadership

**Mary Kay Whitaker
and Ron Whitaker**

Xcelogic, Inc.

It All Starts With YOU: The Power of Pre-Emptive Leadership
Copyright © 2008 Mary Kay Whitaker and Ron Whitaker
Published by Xcelogic, Inc., Kansas City, MO

All rights reserved. No part of this book may be reproduced (except for inclusion in reviews), disseminated or utilized in any form or by any means, electronic or mechanical, including photocopying, recording, or in any information storage and retrieval system, or the Internet/World Wide Web without written permission from the author or publisher.

This publication is designed to provide accurate and authoritative information in regard to the subject matter covered. It is sold with the understanding that neither the author nor the publisher is engaged in rendering financial, accounting, legal, or other professional services by publishing this book. If financial advice or other expert assistance is needed, the service of a competent professional should be sought. The author and publisher specifically disclaim any liability, loss or risk resulting from the use or application of the information contained in this book.

For more information, please contact:
rwhitaker@xcelogic.com

Book design by:
Arbor Books, Inc.
www.arborbooks.com

Printed in Canada

It All Starts With YOU: The Power of Pre-Emptive Leadership
Mary Kay Whitaker and Ron Whitaker

1. Title 2. Author 3. Leadership

Library of Congress Control Number: 2008923130

ISBN 10: 0-9802158-0-3
ISBN 13: 978-0-9802158-0-9

This book is the outcome of soulmates working together through daunting trials and tribulations, facing formidable fears, and living our dreams through sweat, belief, hard work, and endearing relationships with good friends and clients who have helped us fine tune the Pre-Emptive Leadership System and practice its principles; without their authentic leadership and belief, this book would not be possible.

TABLE OF CONTENTS

PART I: WHAT IS PRE-EMPTIVE LEADERSHIP?

Chapter 1: Build a Foundation 5
How to get out of the reactionary loop

Chapter 2: Establish a Connection...25
Are you talking or are you connecting?

Chapter 3: Resolve Misunderstandings Now 45
Conflict is the one thing in business you can count on

Chapter 4: Know What Makes a Person Tick 63
The missing link—finding their passion and yours

Chapter 5: What Right Looks Like: Clarifying Expectations 81
Clear, direct and honest communication

Chapter 6: Instill Accountability 91
Create a culture of commitment

PART II: WHY YOU SHOULD CHANGE THE WAY YOU LEAD

Chapter 7: Outperforming the Competition 101
From manager to leader

Chapter 8: The Power of Pre-Emptive Decisions 113
Let core values decide

Chapter 9: How to Attract and Keep the Best People 123
Talent and the bottom line

Chapter 10: Doing More of What You Love to Do 133
Breaking free—it is possible

Chapter 11: Stay Ahead of the Curve...145
Sticking with a proven system

Chapter 12: Have Fun, Make Money, and Sleep Well 159
Nothing beats a good night's sleep

PART III: HOW CAN I INFLUENCE OTHERS?

Chapter 13: Believe in Yourself First 167
Lead with "no fear"

Chapter 14: Putting Your Ego Aside 175
The secret to leadership success

Chapter 15: Leverage and Build New Habits................................185
Six core competencies

Chapter 16: Teach, Not Preach 199
Everyone teaches something

Chapter 17: Celebrate Achievements 209
Celebration myths

Chapter 18: *Be* a Pre-Emptive Leader 217
It all starts with you

About Xcelogic...225

PART I

WHAT IS PRE-EMPTIVE LEADERSHIP?

What do you think of when you hear the term "Pre-Emptive Leadership"? To prevent problems? To influence a better result? Exactly! Pre-Emptive Leadership provides a plan for leaders to inspire others to make better choices. It is a six-step system for getting results through people that will change the way you do your job and the way you deal with everyone in your life.

Pre-Emptive Leadership is not fluff, psychobabble or rocket science. It isn't about "being nice" or changing who you are. Nor is it a flavor of the month. Pre-Emptive Leadership is a real, proven system that hundreds of companies have used to propel themselves toward the top of their industries more quickly and at less cost than their competitors—while creating high levels of employee loyalty and satisfaction.

Although you might be familiar with some of the terminology we will use to talk about Pre-Emptive Leadership in this book, we will fine tune the generalities most managers know about leadership and laser in on *how to be* a great leader. Though you might recognize some of the system's concepts or techniques, we're going to show you entirely different ways of using them to get dramatically better results from the people you work with.

There are many people involved in making the system work but in reality, IT ALL STARTS WITH YOU. Are you willing to change your habits to get the results you want, to be more successful than you ever thought you could be? This system is not about getting other people to change, or finding out who is to blame for low productivity. This is about working on who you are and learning how to influence those around you in order to achieve the greatest heights for yourself and the company that employs you.

Think about most of the problems you deal with daily. Most of them revolve around people. If you didn't have "people problems" and problems caused by people, imagine all that you could accomplish. It's possible when you employ Pre-Emptive Leadership.

As you'll see, this isn't just another philosophy that sounds good but is impossible to put into practice. We've taught Pre-Emptive Leadership to thousands of managers. Once they see how simple it is, they don't go back to the old way. Neither will you.

What Keeps Managers from Being Leaders?

Pre-Emptive Leaders are proactive and if you want to keep good people, that's what you have to become. Practically speaking, Pre-Emptive Leadership is a way for managers at all levels to have more fun, make more money and genuinely enjoy working with people.

So what keeps managers from being leaders? People problems: Employees who come to work late or don't show up at all; employees who make mistakes and don't speak up when they don't understand; and, most of all, employees who don't take responsibility for tasks that have been assigned to them. As a manager, how do you respond? If you are like most managers, you probably react to these crises by working longer hours, micromanaging projects and, because you are so busy, appearing to be inaccessible or indifferent.

This is **reactive management**. You can't ever seem to leave the office or the whole thing will fall apart. Reactive management causes a downward turn in productivity, morale and turnover. When you have reactionary management, you lose the good people, and the ineffective people stay.

What reactive managers see as the most productive use of their time (getting the job done) is in reality an enormous waste of productivity because the atmosphere it fosters is so dysfunctional that the same mistakes are made over and over, and most problems are rarely resolved.

It's not that you're a *bad* manager. You think you're doing the right thing. But you're actually using the same skill set to deal with people that you use to deal with equipment, processes, and procedures. The problem is that people don't want to be fixed, managed or told what to do; they want to be led.

If this sounds like what you're going through, consider yourself what we call a reactive manager. You're stuck in a rut that can be hard to get out of. Under pressure from your own managers to produce, you probably feel like you can rarely take a day off, much less take a vacation; you most likely push your employees as hard as you are pushed yourself and, to be honest, they may not like you much for it. The result: Walls are built between managers and employees.

Reactive Manager or Pre-Emptive Leader?

Here are some ways to recognize whether you are a reactive manager or a Pre-Emptive Leader:

- A reactive manager tells, pushes, and provides solutions. A Pre-Emptive Leader asks questions, pulls and gets solutions from people.
- A reactive manager gets "yes" people. A Pre-Emptive Leader attracts committed people.
- A reactive manager gets more to do. A Pre-Emptive Leader creates a team.
- A reactive manager has to stay at the job all of the time. A Pre-Emptive Leader gets to take time off and take a vacation.
- A reactive manager stays in the same position. A Pre-Emptive Leader has choices.
- A reactive manager is stressed out. A Pre-Emptive Leader is engaged in visionary tasks.

- A reactive manager burns out. A Pre-Emptive Leader grows and takes on greater responsibility.
- A reactive manager goes in circles dealing with the same "people problems" over and over. A Pre-Emptive Leader gets results.

Ultimately, it's too hard being a reactive manager; it's much easier to be a Pre-Emptive Leader. That's what this book is going to show you. The results of Pre-Emptive Leadership are the same, whether you are a new supervisor or a CEO. These leaders establish productive relationships with all people, their employees, their bosses, their spouses, and their children. In all aspects of their lives, they have developed into Pre-Emptive Leaders. So will you.

What's Next?

Pre-Emptive Leadership is a six-step system that you will learn to help you eliminate your "people problems." It is a choice you can make to achieve your objectives at a quicker, less costly rate than those who continue to use their old style of reactive management. In our first chapter, you'll learn step one of the Pre-Emptive Leadership System—which is so obvious, you'll wonder why you hadn't thought of it before.

CHAPTER 1

Build a Foundation

Although the importance of establishing trust as a leadership tool is discussed in any number of books, many managers do not view trust as a problem-solving tool because of two factors they must confront in the workplace: priorities and pressure. Managers often feel that their first priority is production and getting the job done, and are under pressure to complete tasks as quickly as possible because that's what their own managers are emphasizing.

Many managers know that trust is important, but there are just too many day-to-day issues to deal with and so trust often gets neglected. Believing that they are getting paid to get results, not to build trust, managers don't always recognize the connection between the two.

Start With Morale

If morale is low in an organization, it will impact productivity. When this happens, reactive managers often make the mistake of trying to tackle the end product instead of getting to the root of the actual problem. That is, instead of looking at *why* morale is low or how they can raise it, they focus on increasing productivity by:

- **Reviewing performance data.** Placing a chart in the work area so that team members can focus on their own performance levels works for goal attainment, but not if the morale is the source of productivity problems. Managers who do this sort of thing believe that if they talk about production numbers every day, it will be enough to take care of low productivity.

- **Redistributing the workload.** Switching team members from one job to another may feel like a fresh solution but, in reality, it may only cause more resentment and low morale. Instead, managers should be looking at lack of trust as a cause of the productivity problems.

- **Setting up an efficiency system.** If business is slow, this may seem like the answer. Although looking at inefficiencies is a positive move, the results will only be a temporary fix if trust is lacking in the workplace.

- **Blaming individual workers.** When faced with one employee who seems to be frustrating everyone else, instead of trying to develop the employee or communicate with him directly, the reactive manager often makes excuses for why he can't. "That's just how he is," the manager might say, as though he can do nothing about it. "We just have to work around him."

Any of these four actions will be short-term Band-Aids for the real problem of low morale, which can be like a wound that refuses to heal. In reality, managers need to pay close attention to this phenomenon because though it may seem like just a matter of unhappy employees, low morale goes beyond that superficial level. When team members are unmotivated and unhappy with their work, often it is because there is no foundation of trust in their workplace.

A Different Approach

When it comes to building trust among the team, Pre-Emptive Leaders look at the situation differently than other managers. They know that the people in the organization drive its productivity and success; they also know that if they aren't looking at change within themselves, then they aren't going to get long-term results.

So instead of simply reviewing data and trying to make changes based on cold, hard numbers, Pre-Emptive Leaders first look at themselves. Which of their own behaviors make the team's members want to increase their productivity? How can they, as leaders, engage the hearts and minds of their people? One goal of Pre-Emptive Leadership is to build a team that is empowered instead of disengaged. The first challenge, then, is to figure out how to do that.

Instead of relying on spreadsheets to dictate the direction of their business, Pre-Emptive Leaders look toward people issues when seeking to implement change. First, they try to see how they are engaging with their employees. While reactive managers are in their offices setting up systems, Pre-Emptive Leaders are out seeking the opinions of their team members. They know that in order to get results, they must have the interest, investment and trust of those who are responsible for producing them.

Trust Is Number One

What keeps managers from building trust? One common stumbling block is simply the word "trust." In many organizations, it's so overused that team members don't even seem to know what it means anymore. What's worse, they often do not see trust in action; they've never had anybody teach them how to make it happen for themselves.

Ironically, although trust is one of the most common core values that companies aspire to, if you walked into any given workplace, you would rarely see managers trying to establish trust among their employees. Instead, you're more likely to hear statements such as, "I don't know if I trust him to do that," "I want a guarantee that she's going to do this," and "I've got to follow up and check on them."

These are typical assertions that managers make when talking about their own employees and although they may think that they're doing the right thing for all involved, all this overbearing attitude accomplishes is alienation and an absence of loyalty. In trying to manage their employees the way they would manage processes and procedures, many reactive managers are actually pushing their employees away, and creating teams who don't buy into what they're being asked to do.

When this is the general atmosphere in the workplace, the results can be disastrous. Productivity will undoubtedly suffer, and what will be left for the reactive manager to do is keep tabs on his employees—in essence, to baby-sit them instead of helping them learn and grow.

This pattern can become a vicious cycle if managers are not careful and that is often how a reactive environment takes hold. But there is a way to break it! To get out of the reactionary loop and begin to build a foundation of trust, managers must match their actions to their words and diligently display, in their own leadership style, four expectations of trust: 1) Be approachable; 2) Accept responsibility; 3) Practice confidentiality; and 4) Mutually support all.

> *When team members choose to confide in you, they are taking a big step toward showing that they trust you*

Be Approachable

Start being approachable today and see what kind of response you receive—all you have to do is make yourself available. Let your employees know that you are there for them when they have problems, concerns or questions, and when they do come to you, don't take your own baggage into the conversation. Listen to what they have to say then react logically rather than emotionally.

This sounds a lot easier than it actually is for many people. When we hear something we disagree with, it's a natural reaction to raise our voices and disagree. However, as Pre-Emptive Leaders, we must instead stay calm, open and understanding of the other person's point of view.

We must continue to listen rather than interrupt, shoot the messenger or try to explain away whatever the problem might be.

When team members choose to confide in you, they are taking a big step toward showing that they trust you; they are helping you to start building that foundation. Whatever the topic might be, whatever issue they have decided to bring to you, wait for them to finish their thoughts before you say anything, and make sure that your response is not reactionary. Think things through before you say them; you'll be surprised at how this one small action can turn the tide of any heated conversation.

Many of our clients take this first step and come back to us saying, "Wow, this works!" As a practice, reacting calmly may not come naturally to you right away, especially if you've been a reactive manager for a while. But try it. And stick with it. It won't take long before it will work for you, too.

Accept Responsibility

When we're feeling under pressure ourselves, it's easy to try to throw the blame for whatever problems exist onto somebody else. We can complain about people in other departments or locations; it's better when they're not around to defend themselves. We can also blame our own team members if we have to—for not following through, not meeting deadlines, not returning phone calls or not sharing work-related information.

But all this finger pointing will do is divide your organization and promote fear amongst your employees. Although reactive managers often feel pressured to blame someone or to find a culprit for the low productivity their organizations are experiencing, it is never the best course of action.

Pre-Emptive Leaders know that playing the "blame game" will get them nowhere but deeper into the vicious cycle, and so instead will take ownership of whatever problems arise. When confronted by a difficult issue, these leaders will first stop and ask themselves, "What can I do to rise above the circumstances?" They'll look at themselves first, review their own actions and habits, and proceed to change whatever's necessary to achieve better results.

Often, during this self-examination, Pre-Emptive Leaders find that their first shortcoming is not sharing enough information with their employees. Perhaps they unwittingly held back pertinent details that caused the production process to go less smoothly than it otherwise might have. While this would be a prime time for a reactive manager to blame the slowdown on his employees despite it being largely his fault, Pre-Emptive Leaders instead approach their employees directly and say, "You know, I think there's something that I failed to tell you. Maybe that's why we didn't get that particular project completed on time."

This sort of behavior will undoubtedly feel refreshing to team members that are used to reactive managers, who would normally just say, "I didn't have to tell you—you should have known." Reactive managers point fingers at everyone else; they want to be right and will avoid admitting that they made a mistake at all costs. All of that defensiveness and posturing promotes fear—which is the opposite of trust.

> *All of that defensiveness and posturing promotes fear—which is the opposite of trust*

Practice Confidentiality

Every organization has a rumor mill, whether it wants one or not. Gossip is generated by team members reacting with fear to unfavorable situations. People are generally afraid to go directly to the source of a problem to confirm fact or fiction and decide for themselves what is true. Lacking this pertinent information, they jump to conclusions and create conspiracies when, in actuality, there's nothing there.

Pre-Emptive Leaders have the ability to stop the rumor mill in its tracks by being the role models their team members need. Instead of listening to gossip or passing on potentially false information, leaders go directly to the source to find out the truth about what happened. When other team members see this taking place, they will be encouraged to do the same—with each other and with the leaders as well.

In training sessions, we often ask participants: "If I had a concern about your participation in this session, would you want me to come to you directly and tell you about it, or would you rather I go tell your boss?" The answer is always unanimous: They would rather we approach them directly to discuss the situation.

Our next question is, "What if I told your boss and didn't go to you? How would that affect our trust?" Again, there is a unanimous answer: There would be no trust between us.

Reactive managers often get caught in this sticky situation; they are prone to spreading rumors about co-workers, distracting others with unfavorable perceptions and projecting double standards in the workplace. Unfortunately, it is impossible to earn the trust of your team if you're actively participating in the rumor mill.

On the other side, by repeating only productive information—no rumors or gossip—and communicating directly with those who are involved in the situation at hand, Pre-Emptive Leaders establish trust with their team members. They know that they must practice confidentiality to be an example of trust, and to earn the respect of others.

Mutually Support All

There is no chain of command when it comes to building trust; in this case, the playing field is level. Everyone deserves to be trusted regardless of your position or theirs.

Pre-Emptive Leaders are well aware of this, and so they make sure that they interact with all of their team members equally, and support one employee's efforts just as much as the next one's. It takes everyone to get results, and everyone must feel that sense of equality and trust if you want them to be motivated to succeed.

This may not be the scenario you're used to if you've spent a long time in a reactive environment. Reactive managers tend to work more on their relationships with their bosses than with their team members; often, they seem to have no patience or time for those people they supervise. This attitude comes across as phony, and employees can see right through it; the result is a lack of respect for the manager and a loss of credibility.

Reactive managers, however, don't see it in quite the same way. "These people report to me," they'll argue. "I'm stressed out enough—what do you want me to do?" They focus on their own egos, caring only about themselves to the point that they destroy whatever trust might have existed.

But Pre-Emptive Leaders know that it's smarter to focus on what's best for the team, not what's best for themselves. They are outwardly focused and flexible, willing to help anyone on their team who needs a hand—as well as teams in other areas of the organization.

As an example, consider a successful branch office in an organization that is achieving top results. Because they are doing so well for themselves, the Pre-Emptive Leaders at this branch are eager to share their techniques and practices with other branches in order to help the organization as a whole. Compare this to reactive branch managers, who would keep all the information to themselves, scared that if they share it, they run the risk of being knocked out of first place. As a result, the organization suffers.

In order for an organization to be successful, everyone must feel as though they have a stake in the outcome of their work. This begins with trust—which you can't expect team members to feel if you play favorites or put your own ego first. Mutual support will earn you mutual trust, and that's what it takes to get results.

Putting It All Together

Think for a moment about the people within your organization whom you trust. The odds are excellent that these people exhibit all four of the trust expectation behaviors we discussed above: being approachable, accepting responsibility, practicing confidentiality and mutually supporting all.

But do you? Try putting all four of them to work right now and you will see a difference—possibly even before the day is over.

In order to test your leadership skills, let's go through an exercise that we use in our training sessions. Think of an employee with whom you've had problems; for this example, we'll call her Jane. Could it be that Jane does not work to her full potential because she doesn't trust

Build a Foundation 13

you? Let's go through the four expectations of trust and see what the cause of Jane's problem may be.

- Have you been **approachable** to Jane? Are you as receptive to her as you are to other employees? Do you greet her in the morning? Or, like the reactive manager, do you avoid her because she annoys you?

- Have you accepted **responsibility** for the fact that *you* might be part of Jane's problem? Look at your own actions: What could you be doing differently with her? Do you blame her when things go wrong, even if it's not entirely her fault? Are you focusing on helping her succeed? Or are you just focused on her next vacation, when she'll be out of your hair for a week?

- Have you been practicing **confidentiality** with Jane, or do you complain about her to others? Reactive managers will bad-mouth others. Are you guilty of this bad habit?

- Do you **support** Jane as much as you do everybody else on the team? Do you give her the same amount of work? Do you provide her with the same resources that you would another employee?

When using this checklist, many of our clients realize that they are not practicing the four expectations of trust with difficult employees. When they change their behaviors, however, and concentrate more on being accountable, responsible, confidential and supportive, they begin to see results right away.

What about you? Are you ready to do some self-examination and change the way you deal with your more challenging employees? Take the first step—try changing the way you interact with Jane. You may be amazed by the result.

Why Employees Don't Speak Up

If you're a receptive, attentive leader, chances are employees like Jane will have no problem coming to you with their concerns. When employees approach you so freely, you can pretty much rest assure that you are an excellent Pre-Emptive Leader, and have a great relationship with the people you lead.

But what if your team members *don't* want to talk to you? What if they don't trust you? Would they risk speaking up to a supervisor they have no faith in?

Probably not, and therein lies the problem that must be solved: If your employees don't trust you enough to talk to you about what's wrong, how will you ever know?

In the Pre-Emptive Leadership System, there are methods for soliciting feedback from your employees. One good way is to call them all into a meeting, and ask for their input on how to fix a problem or deal with a change, or gather their opinions on efficiency issues. This works well if there is a good foundation of trust already in place, but if your team members sense a lack of support on your part—and fear reprisal for anything they might say that contradicts you—they will not give you the feedback you need. Although they may know what is not working in the company, they will not say so unless the relationship they have with you is solid, built on a proven framework of reliability.

> *Reactive managers fail to earn trust in part because they try to supervise team members in the same detached way that they deal with equipment and procedures*

The Bicycle Analogy

Reactive managers fail to earn trust in part because they try to supervise team members in the same detached way that they deal with equipment and procedures. They use a cut-and-dried, black-and-white, very structured approach, telling people what to do and making demands instead of soliciting feedback and encouraging their employees to trust them.

Build a Foundation

If you're really good at tasks, processes and the procedures of your job, you may find it difficult to find a good balance between managing and leading. You may put too much emphasis on the former and too little on the latter; maybe you just don't see the importance of constantly switching back and forth between being a manager and leading. The problem is that in order to create a culture that emphasizes success, you must find a way to strike a balance between the two.

Let's look at a bicycle as an analogy of this balance between leadership skills and management skills. The bike's front wheel is the people side of the business, which deals with attitude, cooperation, communication, conflict, interaction and motivation. It's spontaneous, and it's the way you communicate and interact with others to get the job done. All of these skills require leading instead of managing.

The back wheel is the task side, consisting of procedures, policies, job responsibilities, final decisions, roles and compensation. It's more structured than the front wheel; it's your technical expertise, and what you do for a living. These areas require management skills.

As on a bicycle, both wheels must work together in order for you to get anywhere, although each does have its separate purpose. The back wheel is what you use to keep the workplace up and running, but the front wheel is how you steer your way through it. You need to put your team members and their concerns first, to an extent, before all the other technical matters, like job descriptions and company policy. When you do that successfully, back wheel issues will almost resolve themselves; members of your team will follow those policies independently, and you won't need to take time out of your day to remind them.

The problem with this, we've found time and time again, is that reactive managers tend to use their back wheel skill set to solve front wheel "people problems"—in other words, they try to force "people issues" into the "management" mold. They attempt to policy and procedure the problem out of existence, when what they really need to do is just sit down and listen to what an employee has to say—and then figure out a solution together.

The front and back wheels—your leadership and management skills—each have their own distinct characteristics and purpose. Front wheel leadership behaviors may be described as having:

- A focus on relationships
- A personable demeanor
- Spontaneity
- A willingness to share
- Concern for bringing out the best in others
- An ability to describe feelings
- Trust
- Openness to discussing opposing ideas
- An ability to follow gut feelings
- A willingness to share information

Back wheel managerial behaviors when interacting with people may come across to others as having:

- A focus on role
- Expertise in tasks, processes and procedures
- Skepticism
- A guarded nature
- Perfectionism
- Evaluative methods
- A fearful attitude
- Caution
- Controlling habits
- A desire to be the expert
- Independence

These back wheel behaviors work well and are imperative when managing tasks or processes, but will not serve you well when leading people. Why? Because the incorrect skills or tools are being used for a front wheel "people situation." For example, it is like using a bat to play golf, or a hammer when you need a saw. The outcome is not productive and will not provide you the results you need.

Build a Foundation

Both wheels—and all their characteristics—are important, but you need to be certain that you are matching the appropriate skill set to the situation at hand. Reactive managers will approach "people problems" the way they would faulty equipment—by trying to "fix" them, by trying to hammer them into submission, as it were. Reactive managers believe that by throwing enough rules and executive decisions around, they will cause their employees to just back down in fear.

The message sent by a manager who handles situations that way is clear: *Don't make waves. If you're having a problem, fix it yourself, but don't bother me because what do I need you for?* Can you imagine how that would make employees feel? Do you think that they would be loyal toward such a supervisor? Do you think there will be *trust*?

There is—when managers use their front wheel skill set to solve "people issues," and when they stop talking and start listening.

Pulling Versus Pushing

Reactive managers who don't allow team members to express their concerns are said to be *pushing* their own ideas onto everyone else. By doing this, they're sending out the message that there is only one way to do things: theirs. No other opinion or concern is considered.

Pre-Emptive Leaders, on the other hand, *pull* instead of push. It's not that they're yanking their employees by their collars; they're just setting the conditions right so that employees can see the logic and appeal of decisions by themselves. They're setting up an opportune situation, sharing good information, and gently leading their team members in the right direction.

With the pull method, a Pre-Emptive Leader will say, "Hey, some of you are going to have to work this weekend." This may seem like a real blow to employees when they first hear it—who wants to have to work on the weekend unexpectedly?—but the leader knows that by stating the unpopular decision first, he will be able to pull his people in a productive direction. First, he must let them react; then, he can solicit their opinions and ideas, and work together with them to come up with a solution.

The push method, on the other hand, calls for the reactive manager to tell the employees what they have to do without any discussion.

"If you don't come in on Saturday," the manager may state, "don't bother coming in on Monday!" When this is the attitude the supervisor presents to the team, its members will resent the pushing, and will push right back. Even if they agree with the decision—mostly because they *have* to—they may rebel by becoming unproductive, simply because they don't like being told what to do.

Instead of forcing decisions or information on your team members, try using the pull process to get them to *want* to do things that need to be done. You'll know immediately whether or not a team member is onboard and, chances are, if they trust you, they will be. By allowing them to be a part of developing the solution, you'll create a sense of commitment, and in the end you will more likely see the results that you need.

> *Organizations that are successful are learning organizations—they not only believe in engaging their people but in developing them*

The Learning Curve

All leaders want their team members to perform, but it's not always a straight path to such results. Understanding the learning curve can help you lead your team to great achievements by structuring conversations according to a proven pattern.

In today's competitive world, organizations that are successful are learning organizations—they not only believe in engaging their people but in *developing* them. Toward this end, Pre-Emptive Leaders use a learning curve when working with their teams to present priorities and tasks in such a way that the information will stick.

When it comes to the curve, we've found that people learn in four stages:

- NORM: their current mindset
- STORM: their initial reaction
- FORM: the light bulb goes on
- PERFORM: they get it done

NORM

To get results, you must work with your team members' NORMS, or their point of view—something that reactive managers rarely do. Often, they're so focused on their own attitudes and mindsets that they don't ever find out what someone else thinks, much less what they know or believe to be true.

"I've got an announcement to make," a reactive manager might say. "We're switching the time we come to work next week. Let me tell you about it." As the manager speaks on this subject, team members grow more and more anxious, thinking of all the reasons why this sudden change will not work for them. After the manager is through explaining the entire thing, he then thinks to ask, "So, does anyone have any questions?" and everyone looks at him in silence. "Okay," he concludes. "Then let's do it."

This, to a reactive manager, has been a good meeting. To everyone else, the communication has not broken the surface level. Out of touch with what his own employees think—and showing them that he really doesn't even care—he has forced the communication away from himself and into the hallways and restrooms, and has put the rumor mill into action.

Finding out about your employees' NORMS, however, can turn a situation like this right around. All you have to do is ask some questions: "Starting next week, we have to start coming an hour earlier. What do you all think about that?" Pre-Emptive Leaders invite the input that reactive managers actively avoid, knowing that it's the only way to get the support of the team—especially when the topic is a difficult one.

STORM

Once the question ("What do you all think about that?") is out there then comes the STORM, which is the natural reaction most people have when you try to introduce them to change. Even though you may listen to your employees' problems and come up with solutions that you think are for the best, chances are that the team will resist by coming up with reasons why your resolutions won't work. They'll express frustration and confusion; they'll complain and ask questions of their own.

It's important, however, to let them ride this STORM out. It's not your job to stop it! If you don't let team members communicate their thoughts and feelings, you will plug their learning curves; you'll make it clear to them that you don't want to hear what they're thinking and feeling and, in return, they will lose the trust and respect they feel for you. This is the fate of the reactive managers who frequently plug their team members' thoughts and feelings during this STORM phase; for Pre-Emptive Leaders, this is rarely the case.

Pre-Emptive Leaders will not run away from the STORM but will stay and listen, and let it all play out. Employees won't feel safe if they're not allowed to STORM, and they feel even better when they see their leader has not been scared away.

FORM

To FORM means to understand, to commit to a plan. It is during this stage that the proverbial light bulbs will turn on over your team members' heads as they begin to come up with their own solutions to the problem at hand.

This aspect of the FORM phase is important because as humans, we remember little of the information we are supposed to absorb—especially when someone is dictating it to us. Some studies have shown that we only retain 20% of what we write, 20% of what we hear and 20% of what we see.

However, we remember 80% of what we say and do ourselves, so it stands to reason that it's most effective to allow your team members to become involved in the solution-forming process. Hands-on involvement makes a lasting impression on our brains. In short, if you want your employees to *hear* what you're saying, you do the talking; if you want them to really *learn* it, they need to do the talking.

PERFORM

Once your team members have formed their own solutions, they will be ready to move ahead and PERFORM the way you want them to. If you allow them to follow this learning curve—from beginning to end, without interruptions or shortcuts—you will

Build a Foundation

achieve ongoing, sustained results, and add another layer to your foundation of trust.

So why don't all managers do this if it's so effective? Mostly because they fear the process itself. The NORM, STORM, FORM, PER-FORM learning curve creates a lot of energy as it goes along, to the extent that many reactive managers would not be able to contain it. Instead, they would revert to their old skill set that tells them to defend themselves against the opposition, to prove the employees wrong and crush their efforts to resolve the problem in their own way.

When you let your team members express themselves, even the ones who oppose you most will become your greatest advocates

But with Pre-Emptive Leadership, that's not the way it's done. All that the members of your team want you to do is communicate and listen; it's up to you to keep those lines open to hear whatever they have to say. In return, they will give you their best ideas, their most honest efforts; they will see that you are ready to trust them because you have created commitment and buy-in—you have shown your employees that you personally value their expertise, and that you expect them to be just as invested in the outcome as you are.

When you let your team members express themselves, even the ones who oppose you most will become your greatest advocates.

The Learning Curve Gets Results

When you present a potentially unpopular idea to your team, the reaction you're most likely to get across the board is, "This will never work." But instead of being reactive and attempting to sell your employees on the idea of liking the change, you must instead listen to their concerns. As the Pre-Emptive Leader, you must stop and say, "Yes, it is different. And how is that going to affect us?"

And then, again, you must listen. As you do so, take the time to engage each team member; listen actively, and when they're done, paraphrase what they've just told you: for example, "So your concern is transportation, Mary," or "You have child-care issues, Mark." This shows your team members that you're really *hearing* what they're saying, and shows that you're trying to work *with* them, not against them.

Pre-Emptive Leaders encourage their team members to fully participate in the learning curve process and, in fact, jump right in and STORM along with them. Leaders listen to everything their employees say without trying to fix their problems right away, but once the STORM dies out—when people start repeating themselves—and the conversation turns toward the FORM mode, the leaders can ask questions such as: "What can we do to make this unpopular change work out?" and "What are we going to do when we leave here?" Then they add, "Let's go do it."

The learning curve is a powerful tool to use when announcing change to wary team members. It can also be used for a number of other tasks, including communicating unpopular decisions or relieving tensions between team members. Ultimately, the learning curve allows you to structure any conversation so that the recipients of your message have a chance to react, form their own solutions and perform the very thing you had hoped they would do all along.

Take this leadership tool you've just learned and put it to use in your very next conversation. If you change only the way you interact with one or two of your employees to start, or alter how you react to challenging questions in a staff meeting, you'll see immediate results. Once you've established trust, you have a great start toward resolving most of your "people problems."

In a Nutshell

If you can't understand why someone's not doing what you want them to, look at yourself first and figure out if you are the cause of their hesitancy. Use the checklist to see if you are conforming to the four expectations of trust:

1. Am I being approachable?
2. Have I accepted responsibility?

Build a Foundation

3. Am I practicing confidentiality?
4. Am I mutually supportive of the person I consider difficult?

If your answer to any of these questions is "no," take immediate steps to change them to "yes." Stop talking, and ask more questions; really listen to what your employees have to say. You do not need to fix or solve their problems right away, and often listening to them first will help the solution present itself.

When presenting change or difficult decisions to your team, utilize the learning curve tool and guide them through the NORM, STORM, FORM and PERFORM stages. Remember that it's okay for there to be initial resistance; the most important part is creating a connection and coming to a solution together as a team.

What's Next?

You may think that your employees are listening to you, but are you sure that they're hearing what you're saying? In the next chapter, we'll take a look at different styles of communication, and how you can adjust yours to make sure that you're understood—and get results.

CHAPTER 2

Establish a Connection

Once you've used the tools in the last chapter to establish trust, most of your "people problems" will be resolved. However, this does not mean that your productivity will magically increase. Even when the trust is there, results might not come exactly as you need them. And the cause of this may be ineffective communication.

When we meet with potential clients, the first thing we always hear is, "If we could all just communicate effectively, we could accomplish anything!" Most organizations, in our experience, feel the same way— that the number one problem with employees is communication.

But what organizations think is a lack of communication is often something else entirely. Unresolved conflicts, unequipped or untrained team members, or even employees who are unable to perform their jobs correctly can all disguise themselves as poor communication issues at one time or another. The problem for Pre-Emptive Leaders, then, is to decide when communication truly is or is not the cause of a problem, and how to avoid the mistakes that limit effectiveness.

Are You Talking—or Are You Connecting?

Communication is based on two elements: how one delivers a message, and how the receiver processes it. If you fail to get your point across effectively, you fail to get the other person's attention, causing them to disconnect from the interaction. When this happens, the communication is incomplete; the receiver does not receive the message you intended to send, much less process it and act on it accordingly.

When a disconnect in communication spreads into the workforce, it runs the risk of impacting the entire company

As an example, how many times have you encountered people who talk too slowly or too rapidly, who provide too much detail or not enough? Do you hear them? Do you process their messages? When the method of delivery is just too confusing or boring, you may be physically there but often you're mentally gone. As your conversation partner jabbers along on autopilot, your attention wanders, and you start thinking about what you'll do next or where you'll go for lunch instead of really listening. When you find yourself wondering when the person speaking to you is ever going to finish his speech, in short, the two of you are not connecting.

Miscommunication occurs when one person doesn't deliver a message in the same manner as the other person processes it. As we see in the example above—and have undoubtedly experienced in our own lives—some of us deliver our thoughts more rapidly than others; on the other end, some receive the messages more slowly.

When this disconnect in communication occurs between yourself and members of your team, the results can be disastrous. If you don't hear their messages, you will not take any action to remedy whatever their problems are, and this can erode the trust you may have established with your employees. After this, they will think twice about coming to you with questions or concerns; they may feel alienated, leading to a lack of trust and motivation. In time, this "simple" case of poor communication can impact the whole department.

And it's possible for it to even go beyond that. When a disconnect in communication spreads into the workforce, it runs the risk of impacting the entire company by creating a reactive environment based on fear and mistrust. In the worst-case scenario, dysfunctional departments become isolated from other parts of the organization, and the result is a major communication breakdown.

An example of this is a clash occurring between an employee of the HR department and an employee from another department. Because these two employees fail to make a communicative connection, uneasiness grows between them and they begin to avoid each other in the workplace.

This disconnect means that people are not getting the information they need—that potentially vital details are not being exchanged between HR and the other department. When this happens, the HR department is essentially working without feedback or direction—just going down its own path with little guidance from a much-needed resource.

Based on a simple lack of connection between two employees, this situation shows how easily the departments within an organization can become disconnected—and how easily it could be resolved if everyone could just be trained to communicate with each other more effectively. Within a reactive environment, however, the solution often comes more in the form of a policy or procedure handed down by management on how everyone else must communicate with HR. What is needed, instead, is a way to get employees speaking each other's language.

It's Not Just What You Say; It's How You Say It

Many managers do not know how to effectively communicate them-selves—much less how to teach their employees to do it. Reactive managers are known to deliver messages the way they operate the cruise control on their cars: at one speed, in one way, with no devia-tion. In other words, they use the method they like (though not necessarily one that works) and they stick with it.

But when you do this, you will connect with only a certain percent-age of the population you're trying to reach; instead of everyone in the department hearing your message, it will come across only to those who process the same way you do. In this way, the cruise-control approach limits your opportunities to connect with a large and varied audience.

Imagine a salesperson who can communicate with only a small percentage of his clients—only those who are exactly like him. Imagine how much more productive he would be if he could adjust his style of communication so that a wide variety of customers could understand his pitch.

Now, consider the team members you manage who don't respond to what you have to say. How could you package your communication to make it more understandable to these hard-to-reach people?

First, take a look at your pace—at how rapidly or slowly you speak. This is the first element that determines whether or not your message gets heard. If you're talking too fast and the people you're addressing can't keep up, they miss your message. If you're dragging it out, they'll become bored and lose focus. The key is to understand your audience. By slowing down or speeding up your speech, you can be assured that as many people as possible will process your message.

The second element that will determine if your message is understood is your priority—that is, whether you choose to address front wheel *people topics* or back wheel *task topics*. Managers have been trained to be all about the back wheel; when they have something to say, they stick to communicating only the subject matter. This makes the message more palatable for those team members who process information better when it's to the point.

Leaders, on the other hand, know when to add front wheel *people topics* and phrases to the back wheel message. They ask their team members how things are going before bringing up the issue at hand, and take time out of their busy days to have social exchanges. They know that if they don't cater to this personal side of the workplace, they will lose the trust of those team members who process messages better with some interactive conversation.

What it comes down to is that people are actually a lot like computers: We need the right input to make a successful connection. An employee who processes people-oriented phrases needs a social exchange in order to connect. An employee who processes task-oriented communication needs to hear just what's expected of him. If either of these types doesn't get what he needs, he will tune out and disconnect from the conversation—and your message will never get through.

Establish a Connection

Communication Styles

FASTER-PACED

FRONT-WHEEL PRIORITY

BACK-WHEEL PRIORITY

Style: Faster-Paced Front-Wheel

*Communicate **Acceptance** to Connect*

Processes: Social greetings with positive, forward-looking statements

Needs to work on:
Organizing their thoughts, they tend to over promise (in the head, out the mouth); needs to provide clarity and details

Disconnects for this style:
1. Arguing with them
2. Avoiding them
3. Talking about problems
4. They don't process negative statements

Connections for this style:
1. Favorable recognition
2. Spend time with them; make them a priority
3. Ask for their ideas and solutions
4. Communicate what you want - not what you don't like

Style: Faster-Paced Back-Wheel

*Communicate **Results** to Connect*

Processes: Brief statements that get to the subject at hand

Needs to work on:
Patience; when communicating to others, listening skills (tends to selectively listen); needs to reduce fidgety body language

Disconnects for this style:
1. Telling them what to do
2. Critiquing personal habits
3. Proving them wrong
4. Too much verbiage

Connections for this style:
1. Talk about challenges (things to fix)
2. Support their goals/ideas
3. Get to the point; show results
4. Be assertive with them not aggressive

Style: Slower-Paced Front-Wheel

*Communicate **Reassurance** to Connect*

Processes: Stability statements followed by genuine interest in what they think

Needs to work on:
Opening up and expressing their ideas (they tend to not speak up and communicate what they are thinking)

Disconnects for this style:
1. Overwhelming them with too much information or talking
2. Abrupt or intense communication
3. Finishing their sentences
4. Insincere compliments

Connections for this style:
1. Ask them questions instead of telling
2. Appeal to their personal life situations
3. Give them new information first
4. Provide information in bite-size pieces

Style: Slower-Paced Back-Wheel

*Communicate **Accuracy** to Connect*

Processes: Written communication that is precise and factual

Needs to work on:
Interacting with people (prefers to work alone, intense with others, workaholic, introvert)

Disconnects for this style:
1. Criticizing their work
2. Face-to-face conversations
3. Shooting from the hip; not knowing your facts
4. Starting with social exchanges

Connections for this style:
1. Give them the credit
2. Provide accurate statements
3. Discuss options, alternatives
4. Let them be the expert; ask for expertise

SLOWER-PACED

Communication Style

It's important to understand that your communication style is not your personality; it's simply the way you deliver and process messages. It's your *language*.

There are four basic communication styles that we use when we communicate with one another: faster-paced with a back wheel priority; faster-paced with front wheel priority; slower-paced with front wheel priority; and slower-paced with back wheel priority. Usually, only one out of ten people is fluent in all four of them; most of us tend to take a little bit from each, and create our own unique, blended style.

Let's take a look at each of these communication styles.

Faster-paced with a back wheel priority

People who prefer this "language" are task-oriented. They process messages rapidly in task-related language, but don't always catch all of the details. They focus in on the bottom right corner of any spreadsheet or contract—where the totals and sums are located. They truly are bottom-line communicators.

These are the questions in the heads of fast-paced communicators: What do you want? What do you need? Why are we doing this? How are we doing this? What are the end results?

When engaged in a conversation, they may shoot off rapid-fire queries such as the ones above in an effort to get to the facts; as a result, they're perceived as being too abrupt. When you're talking to them, they process only two to three words per sentence, all they hear is the purpose, process and payoff of your message.

As communicators, these team members may fidget, over-talk you, interrupt or even finish your sentences. Since they cannot process your language, these are the only ways that they can respond to what you're saying.

Team members who espouse a conflicting communication style will have problems communicating with a fast-paced/back wheel communicator. They'll think of this person as too abrupt, rude, cranky or insensitive—a logical conclusion because when confronted with communicators from any of the other three styles, these fast back wheelers either disconnect from or take over the conversation. They come across as intimidating. It's a difficult language for team members that are not skilled in this style to communicate with.

In our training program, we teach managers how to communicate with this language. It's been misused and misinterpreted; team members often confuse this style of communicator as being highly effective with back wheel methods and processes. For some reason, if you're to-the-point and don't make a lot of chitchat with your co-workers, you're often perceived as being more effective than someone else; of course, this is just a perception, and not the truth.

Disconnects: They'll tune you out if you tell them what to do, criticize their personal habits or prove them wrong.

How to connect: These communicators respond best when you talk about challenges, support their goals and ideas, get to the point, show results and are assertive but not aggressive.

Attention-getting terms:
"Do it"
"Goals"
"Results"
"Accomplish"
"Bottom line"
"Here's the deal"
"Progress"

Faster-paced with front wheel priority

This language is very spontaneous. The speaker begins each interaction with a social greeting and chitchat, and then transitions to the topic that needs to be discussed. This type of communication involves asking for ideas and best processes positive statements like targets, goals and solutions; this language doesn't like to hear about what's not working.

Communicators who fall under this category are frequently jumping to conclusions. They will swear that they told you something that never came out of their mouths—probably because they're thinking so fast, they can't remember what they said.

Those who do not process this language tend to view this style of communicator as fluffy or of little substance. They leave the conversation thinking, *Did they really understand what I was saying? Will they follow through? Is this for real? Where does all this chitchat come from?*

This particular language is the most misunderstood because it does not process negatives. While the listeners filter out the word "deadline," they will understand and respond to "target"—a friendlier, more positive way of saying "deadline."

But it takes a Pre-Emptive Leader to understand this nuance, and to communicate effectively with people of this style. Most reactive managers, lacking the patience to deal with this way of talking and listening, perceive its practitioners as wasting time, talking too much and being unable to concentrate.

Those who process in this way tend to have long résumés—that is, they don't spend too long at one job. They're trying to find their "place," an environment where employees and managers are positive and speak their language. Managers that don't understand how to communicate with this language often lose their most creative and talented people.

When faster-paced front wheelers feel threatened, however, all of the positive talk stops. We've seen this in action while consulting at one of our client companies. As part of our job, we had an audience with the CEO, and we explained to him the things that were not working in his company.

"Don't tell me what's not working," he snapped. "Tell me what to do about it!"

This type of response is not unusual with a faster-paced, front wheel communicator. If they don't like what they hear, just like their faster-paced back wheel compatriots, they'll start over-talking you, and become suddenly opinionated and argumentative.

Disconnects: This type will tune you out if you argue with them, avoid them or talk about negative topics.

How to connect: This type responds to favorable recognition. Spend time with them, make them a priority and involve them in creative projects such as problem solving. Communicate what you want—not what you don't like.

Establish a Connection

Attention-getting terms:
"Create"
"Generate"
"Brainstorm"
"Wonderful"
"Target"
"Fabulous"
"Super"
"I've got an idea"

Slower-paced with front wheel priority

If you can't quite figure out what type of processor a team member is, then the answer is probably slower-paced, front wheel. Speakers of this language are often viewed as very difficult to read because they don't express themselves well. They tend to listen too much; although they are excellent listeners, any strength that is overused runs the risk of becoming a weakness.

Because these people are quiet and reserved, other team members talk over them, and they just let it happen. They rarely ask questions, preferring that someone else be in control of the conversation. For the most part, the slower-paced front wheeler keeps quiet and lets others—who don't deal well with silence—tell them what to do, thus perpetuating the softer image that they already project.

Team members who don't process in this manner often feel that the slower-paced, front wheel communicator is amiable, shy and passive—someone who really doesn't have much to offer. They question this communicator's participation level, which is a common misconception.

Disconnects: They'll tune you out if you overwhelm them, communicate abruptly or use competitive topics as a method of clarification.

How to connect: Because speakers of this language best process stability statements, you can engage them with reassurances such as, "Everything is okay," "Let's just start with the first piece" or

"Let's break this into steps." Ask questions about their personal lives or work situation, and let them talk. You can also deal with their strong need for cooperation and harmony by giving them new information first.

Avoid personal compliments with slower-paced front wheelers; they will be perceived as insincere. "You've done a really good job" is a nice thing to say, but if you can turn it into a stability statement such as, "Your team is very effective," it will be much better received.

Attention-getting terms:
"What about…?"
"Will you help?"
"Team"
"We can"
"Everything's okay"
"Share"
"Just a few"

Slower-paced with back wheel priority

People who fall under this category like to communicate by e-mail because it gives them time to process messages and study them in advance. They don't process very easily face to face; they prefer to pore over details, facts, figures and data instead. If people like this are in sales, they will frequently e-mail the decision makers in advance and can even close a sale without having to meet with the prospective client face to face.

To those not speaking their language, slower-paced back wheelers come across as flippant or sarcastic, and they may seem to act like know-it-alls. They tend to isolate themselves; you won't find them out on the floor, interacting with their coworkers. They prefer to be left alone to do their jobs.

If this isn't your language, you may view people like this as distant, and feel as though you're being interrogated every time you interact with them. Because they're very serious about their interactions, people usually use a social exchange to try to lighten them up, but this is the worst thing you can do; trying to reach them on a personal level guarantees that they will not hear you.

These communicators pick up information about people quickly and are excellent people-readers, but they don't see the link between reading team members and getting results; they are inflexible when it comes to changing their own style of communication to meet the needs of their listeners. The way they process is black and white.

Disconnects: They'll tune you out if you criticize their work, deal with them in a "touchy-feely" manner or shoot from the hip without knowing your facts.

How to connect: The best way to communicate is to give them the credit and let them be the expert. Know your stuff, and only go face to face when there's a misunderstanding. It's important to be prepared; whatever you say needs to be accurate. Don't ever communicate something to these individuals that you don't intend to do or that you're not sure is correct. If you do, you're guaranteed an instant disconnect.

Attention-getting terms:
"Review"
"Percentage"
"Options"
"Calculate"
"Quantify"
"Process"
"Analyze"

E-mail caveat: While it is good to use e-mail when communicating with this style of communicator, do not use this method if you have conflict or tension with them, and never respond to e-mail with conflict or tension in it. With any communication style, if it seems like a problem is arising in the electronic format, that's the time to pick up the phone and solve it verbally.

36   It All Starts With YOU

Style-adjust for immediate results

Most of the managers we train discover that they've been using the opposite pace and priority of the team members who have been giving them problems. If this is the case, no wonder you're not being heard!

If you're trying a rapid, back wheel communication approach with someone who processes with a slower, front wheel priority, it's going to create an instant disconnect. You can't just get right to the point with a person who needs substance and details first.

Conversations between the different types of communicators can be difficult sometimes. Often, it seems as though they're not even talking to each other about the same topic! When, for example, a faster-paced, back wheel communicator (A) comes up against a slower-paced, front wheel communicator (B), a dialogue like this is bound to occur:

> A: Just give me a yes or a no answer.
> B: What's the question?
> A: Quit pretending you don't know.
> B: But I *don't* know. What's the subject?
> A: You know what the subject is. Quit trying to act dumb.

As a leader, you cannot afford to get into a situation such as this—you can't be so disconnected when trying to communicate, or not much will get done. But that's what will happen if you do not adjust your style for the person you're talking to: You'll get nowhere, and you'll

It's like giving them glasses so that they can see better; if that's what they need for better results, then that's what you want them to have

be seen as ineffective and annoying. You will be a reactive manager who is not heard, and is thus avoided. Team members will stop listening to you.

On the other hand, if you can adjust to the various communication styles needed from you, you'll be heard. This is not to say that you must change who you are; you just have to accept that the most effective communicators can *temporarily* adjust to the style of the team member to whom they're speaking. Once the connection is made, you'll be on your way to building trust and can soon return to your "cruise control" communication style.

It's important to understand that the technique of style adjusting is not about mirroring or mimicking what the other person is saying. To illustrate, we had a client who worked in sales and thought that if he could get his prospective client to talk about fishing—one of the client's favorite hobbies—he could get him connected, and then make a sale. The salesperson believed that by *mirroring* the interest of the client, he would get the result that he wanted.

But did it get him closer to the sale? Of course not, because the salesperson didn't really understand how the prospective client *processed* their conversation. As he came to learn in our training, his client may not have even *wanted* to chitchat about fishing; he might have wanted just to get down to business.

Mirroring is actually a form of manipulation, of trying to make someone discuss what *you* think will bring about a result that is in your favor. It's not effectively communicating; the message you're conveying is not in the receiver's best interest and this is a duplicity that they will pick up on.

Mirroring and manipulation are two communication methods that are not part of the Pre-Emptive Leadership System. Pre-Emptive Leaders are, of course, concerned with getting results, but they are also aware that they must work for the good of all involved. To them, style adjusting is a means of providing team members with what *they* need in order to get results, without coming across as phony and insincere.

How to Style Adjust

Many managers grasp the concept of style adjusting; what they don't get is just how much it can improve communication and impact results. Once you understand its value, you will be eager to jump right in and do it.

Some think it's phony or manipulative to communicate with team members based on the style of communication they understand, but try to look at it as providing others with the resources and tools they need to get the job done. It's like giving them glasses so that they can see better; if that's what they need for better results, then that's what you want them to have.

But realize as well that this is a temporary adjustment; you are not changing who you are. You are merely shifting to another language for the time being in order to get your point across in a way that people will understand. Think of it as though you're traveling to another country, and utilizing a little of the native tongue; if you go to Germany and speak a little bit of German when ordering your meals, you're going to get the waiter's attention and, hopefully, much better service.

As trust builds with your team members and a connection forms between you and them, you can go back to your "cruise control" style, with the option to switch back and forth between styles as needed. This differs from the approach taken by reactive managers, who rarely go off of the "cruise control" level. They are, no matter the situation, mostly oblivious as to how they come across to others—a trait commonly known as being "unconsciously incompetent."

As a Pre-Emptive Leader, you will have the ability to adjust and connect in a way that is not available to most reactive managers because you are engaged with your team members. This will give you a competitive edge and allow you to focus on what needs to be done because, in the long run, you will have much fewer "people problems" to deal with.

Read a Person in Less Than a Minute

When interacting with your team members, you want to communicate with them in the style they process best. But how are you supposed to know which to choose?

The ability to tell which style a person prefers is what we refer to as "reading" a person—or picking up on the personal traits that can tell you which style they prefer. This can be done very quickly, if you know what to look for:

- Faster-paced communicators *talk* a lot, in a loud tone of voice. They "talk with their hands" and tend to walk around as they speak. Whatever is in their heads comes out of their mouths.

Establish a Connection

- Slower-placed communicators *listen* more than they talk; their speech is often in a soft-spoken monotone, punctuated by pauses. They appear cautious and quiet. When asked a question, they reply with one-word answers; they sometimes squint at the ceiling while talking and keep their arms close to their body.
- Front wheel communicators prefer to talk about events, people, situations, family, friends, stories and experiences.

- Back wheel communicators talk mostly about results, data, processes, procedures, goals and their job.

With managers, it's easy to sense their pace and priority as well. The way in which they ask a team member to complete a task provides a good look into their communication style. Phrases to watch for include:

- "I want it done now." This indicates a faster-paced back wheel communicator.

- "Wow, this is great" is how a faster-paced, front wheel manager might respond.

- "I'd like you to review and quantify this summary and provide me with an analysis of your finding." This is something you might hear from a slower-paced, back wheel communicator.

- "If you could take a minute, this could really help me out" is the slower-paced, front wheel approach.

This could all be one request, but with four very different ways of communicating it.

When "reading" people for their communication style, you first need to know if they're even hearing you. If they're not—indicated by a repeated pattern where you aren't getting results—you need to switch gears, go to the front wheel and determine if you're sending the message in the right way. Then, you can decide if communication is the cause.

Packaging Your Communication

We've already established that not everyone receives messages the same way. So what can you do to reach everyone in a group, and ensure that they are all hearing what you're saying?

We've heard managers ask us many times, "What do I do if I'm sending a message and there are multiple languages present?" The answer that we always give is that you have to try to appeal to all of them—but one at a time, in as orderly a fashion as possible. You don't want to leave anyone out.

As an example, let's say that you're giving a presentation to an audience. The first part of your talk should be geared toward the faster-paced, back wheel audience members. These are the people who need to hear the purpose, process and payoff right upfront. If you start out with front wheel topics and a slow pace, and then try to ease into the topic, you'll lose these people who process faster.

Next, you need to speak to faster-paced, front wheel communicators, who are eager to hear about all of the benefits, the targets and the vision of the project. Third, address your slower-paced, front wheel priority listeners, who need to hear stability statements and a plan for getting started.

In the last part of your presentation, go over all of the details and all of the data, giving everyone a full picture of what needs to be done. Having already heard their own communication language upfront, they now have connected to your message with ease and eagerness.

An example presentation based on this model would sound something like this:

- First (fast-paced, back wheel): "We're changing health insurance starting March 1. The purpose—to provide coverage to all. The project will take three months."

- Second (fast-paced, front wheel): "We envision great things! We anticipate that everyone is really going to like the new opportunities and many possibilities of this new venture."

Establish a Connection   41

- Third (slow-paced, front wheel): "Everything's okay since we have a step-by-step plan. There will be small, transparent changes to the associates in our organization."

- Last (slow-paced, back wheel): "Now, let's review the details of how we're going to implement this project and the analysis and data that support this decision."

We've proven many times in client sessions that this is the best way to present information when there is more than one type of receiver in the audience. You can use this communication model for letters and e-mail as well. Just start with the purpose, process and payoff; move to the benefits and the vision; use the third section to reassure; and, finally, close with all of the details. It's a formula that works to increase communication with a larger number of people.

As a Pre-Emptive Leader, your focus will be connecting with others, but you may not be able to do so in every situation. At times, there will be times when you will go to your employees and say, "Look, I just need this by five o'clock" or, "This has to be completed immediately!" This blatant forthrightness is a communication tool that Pre-Emptive Leaders know to use at the right time for the right reason.

Check Yourself

Are you beginning to see what a major breakthrough this process can be when it comes to the "people problems" in your organization? Most of our clients, when they really start focusing on their communication styles, see results right away—even when they apply these methods to their personal lives. A president of one of our client companies once told us, "It's really working with my kids. In fact, it works better at home than at work—probably because I'm trying harder at home."

Another client told us that he was separated from his wife and was contemplating filing for divorce. Only days after he completed our training, he was back at home "really" communicating with his family.

Once you understand the importance of the connection step and how it prevents "people problems," it will not take you long to implement it in every aspect of your life. You will find yourself no longer making the most common mistakes that managers commit at this point: talking too much without asking questions; over-talking employees who take too long to answer questions; waiting too long to share vital information; and procrastinating when it comes to setting up conversations.

The true measure of whether or not your message is connecting is nothing more than a simple, two-way conversation. Regardless of whether it's fast or slow, it should have a pattern; it should be a 50/50 give and take, with each person contributing value to the conversation.

In a Nutshell

Pre-Emptive Leaders make sure to package their communication so that the majority of people can hear them—especially people with whom they are having problems.

Communication is based on how a message is delivered and how it is received. Miscommunication occurs when one person doesn't deliver information in the same style as the other person processes it.

Your communication style is based on how rapidly you speak and whether you prefer to address front wheel or back wheel priorities. There are four basic communication styles, and in order to be an effective leader, you must be able to switch back and forth between them, as the situation and your team members require, to get the results you want.

When communicating with an audience, it can be difficult to address all the different listening styles in attendance, but it's imperative to do so if you want everyone to get onboard with the ideas you're presenting.

When looking to improve communication in your company, start with yourself. Understand the importance of connecting with your employees and remember that a conversation is only a success when it is a true exchange of ideas—a give and take.

What's Next?

Do you dread conflict in the workplace? As a leader, you must overcome this fear and learn to use conflict constructively. In the next chapter, we will take a look at the Pre-Emptive Leadership tools that will help you teach people to speak up and solve their own problems, instead of letting conflict destroy your team and your organization.

CHAPTER 3

Resolve Misunderstandings Now

Conflict: just the word causes unease in the minds of so many managers who struggle with a fear of confrontation. But could this dread be the product of a larger problem? That's what we've found with many of our clients. They do not know how to solve conflicts productively because they are uncertain about how to start a conversation when the topic is difficult. They are uncomfortable with going directly to team members to discuss a conflict situation because they believe it may get worse.

The same goes for the team members themselves—they avoid conflict and tough conversations, but mostly because they fear hurting people's feelings. So many employees have had unpleasant experiences with this in the past that it inhibits them from acting more effectively.

When Conflict Becomes Emotional

This is often a problem when it comes to the learning curve you were introduced to in Chapter One. When people get stuck in the STORM phase of the curve, their interactions become elevated and managers often don't know how to move the heated discussion toward a productive dialogue. They fear the confrontation because they don't know how to pull out of it and therefore avoid discussions altogether, or become too emotional and react by shouting, and then avoiding the team or isolating themselves. This is what we call "self-defeating behavior."

Our four styles of communication have a lot to do with how a manager reacts to a confrontational situation. When faced with a conflict that has to be resolved, the different communicators will react in the following ways:

For the **faster-paced, back wheel** communicators, conflict is always emotional. They get upset when there is conflict; they shout, and become so frustrated that they assume the worst and blurt out whatever comes to mind without thinking about what they're saying.

The **faster-paced, front wheel** communicators are the pretenders—that is, they pretend that the conflict does not exist. These types just want to move on to something more positive rather than discussing the tension that exists. Their way of handling a tough situation is to retreat by focusing on more pleasant activities.

Slower-paced, front wheel communicators can sit on a problem for years. They are avoiders; they shut down and internalize their frustrations, often affecting their health in the process.

Slower-paced, back wheel communicators tend to isolate themselves when confronted with conflict. They get busy with their work instead of dealing with the problem, often saying things like, "I'll just take care of it myself."

Though none of us like it, conflict itself is essential and one of the few things in business that you can count on. Without it, there can be no progress. Pre-Emptive Leaders understand this and so do not shy away from conflict, no matter what their communication style is; instead, they respond to it productively before it gets out of control.

Pre-Emptive Leaders know that active conflict management increases productivity and performance. Indeed, the key to performance is actively managing the conflict as it arises, and seeing it as a continuous process.

Pre-Empting Destructive Conflict

Conflicts start out small, flare up and then die down; it's a typical destructive cycle that exists in all workplaces. Usually, everyone knows that this conflict cycle exists, but no one knows how to stop it—not even managers, who instead revert to their old, familiar, back wheel skill set and isolate themselves so that they don't have to deal with front wheel "people situations."

Of course, these managers will give excuses for not addressing the destructive conflict—"I'm really, really busy" is a familiar refrain, as is, "I get paid for results, not babysitting." This happens even though, most of the time, it's clear to see which team members are feeding the destructive cycle and keeping it going. Managers simply refuse to deal with it because they do not want to have a confrontation.

But it's a big mistake to avoid situations like this, regardless of how tough they are. Letting the conflict go on unchecked is unfair to your team, and can be costly to your company by affecting results and negatively impacting production. Ignoring the destruction shows that you care mostly about your own interests and are not outwardly focused, which just contributes to the problem.

Pre-Emptive Leaders, conversely, are eager to uncover destructive conflicts and pre-empt them. They know that having tough discussions is the right thing to do and believe in the success of others; they know that without engaging in difficult conversations, team members can't be successful. It is by giving team members an opportunity to solve the conflict that Pre-Emptive Leaders get positive results.

Conversation Map

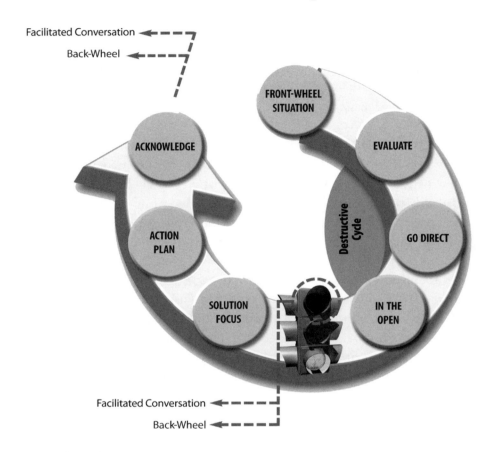

The Conversation Map

When entering unknown territory, it's a good idea to bring along a map, and the same goes for when you're entering a tough conversation. During interactions, a map can ensure that you do not talk about the same misunderstanding more than once and do not skip steps; it also facilitates the energy to move from STORM to FORM and over to PERFORM, the phase in which solutions take place.

A map is a consistent system that works every time. It teaches managers how to communicate with, help and influence each other. It can also teach team members how they can solve difficult situations by themselves in the future.

Resolve Misunderstandings Now 49

Before attempting to use a Conversation Map, you must make sure that the misunderstanding or conflict to be resolved is truly impacting productivity. If team members are just having disagreements amongst themselves that are not affecting the working environment, the conversation map model is not really necessary. This is a tool to be used for larger-scale issues only, ones that are currently impacting productivity and results.

You might believe that you can't really do anything about somebody's attitude, but you can. For example, when an individual's attitude makes team members want to leave the company, that is the time for you to step up and take action. A reactive manager works around this situation by putting off dealing with problem employees and instead saying, "That's just the way they are." Pre-Emptive Leaders, though, don't let anything that affects productivity exist in their workplace or organization.

You can have two types of conversations using a Conversation Map: one-on-one, or a facilitated discussion. Whichever type you choose, the map (see Conversation Map graphic) will chart the difficult but necessary conversation from beginning to end.

Let's look at an example of a time when you might want to utilize the Conversation Map. Say you have a front wheel (people) situation in the workplace that's affecting productivity, and you've determined that one employee—in this case, we'll call him Steve—is slowing everybody else down. Everyone on the team knows this, but no one has felt comfortable enough to go to Steve directly and discuss the situation.

Now, when something like this arises, a manager should be talking to Steve about being a better team member but, in this case, the manager either isn't aware of the problem, or is isolating himself and ignoring it. This is a great opportunity for Pre-Emptive Leaders to step up and take the reins, by following the map in order to reap results.

Using the Conversation Map consists of two steps: evaluating the situation and going directly to the person in question. Let's look at what each step involves:

Evaluate: This phase cannot take more than twenty-four hours; if it does, that means you're procrastinating, and not making the decisions that you need to make in order to go on to the next step. Here, you must ask yourself: Am I too emotional to go to Steve right now? Is the timing right for what's going on in the workplace? Has Steve's behavior been part of a pattern, or is it a one-time occurrence? Ask yourself these questions just to make sure that you're using the map appropriately, at the right time and in the right place.

Go Direct: If you don't go directly to the source of the problem, you'll break down trust; even though many managers know this, they just don't know how to begin the approach. If you've hesitated to have tough conversations because you weren't sure how to start, use the following conversation-starting tool to package your communication into three parts:

- State how you feel about the situation.
- State the topic or behavior.
- End with how the problem impacts the organization.

Example: "Steve, *I* feel upset [situation] when phone calls are not returned [behavior] because the people completing the orders can't get products to the customer [impact]."

It's not unusual to become emotional when discussing issues that can impact the organization, so don't panic if that's how you feel. Just remember that you *can* state your emotions without being emotional, and that you need to be certain to include all three elements when you start the conversation. This will set you on a level playing field with your listeners, and show them that you have the right intentions.

One important word to avoid when starting conversations about problems with your employees is "you." When you make the discussion personal like that, the audience will take it personally, and may be less inclined to hear you out, much less do what you want them to.

As you engage your employees in conversation regarding potentially controversial topics, remember your expectations of trust—specifically, remember to be confidential. Reactive managers will tell others in their department about the problem that one person is causing; Pre-Emptive

Leaders will instead go directly to the employee involved with the motivation to help, not hurt. Leaders focus on being logical, and on having the difficult discussions at the earliest stage possible, when they first sense that tension is affecting productivity.

When reactive managers do finally get around to going directly to the source of the problem, they tend to approach the individual in attack mode, making vague accusations such as, "You haven't returned my phone call." Pre-Emptive Leaders instead start by stating how they feel and choose specific, unbiased phrases as they go, such as, "I tried to reach you a couple of times yesterday." In short, Pre-Emptive Leaders want to help, while reactive managers seek only to punish their wayward team members.

By repackaging your message to be in line with the three steps outlined in the "go direct" topic above, you can really open up a conversation. By further utilizing the conversation map, you can move smoothly from start to finish and end up with result-oriented actions and positive outcomes. Just as a land map helps you move safely from one territory to another, this one will guide you through the conversations that have been a source of anxiety.

The Conversation Map continues with the following steps:

In the Open: When you start conversations with employees, it's important to also listen to what they have to say—to let them move along the learning curve and into the STORM phase of communication. Along with *going direct*, this step makes up the STORM phase of the map and helps to structure how people express themselves and respond. By letting each team member speak while others listen, the conversation will be focused and regulated. The real value of this step is that team members get to hear what they've never heard before—each other's opinions, confusion or complaints. The focus is not on who's right or wrong or what's fact or fiction; the only focus here is getting perceptions out in the open, and getting on to the next step.

Red Light/Green Light: Most people avoid conflict because the STORM is as far as the conversation gets and never goes on to the red light/green light statement, which propels it further along.

When your employee is STORMing but comes to a halt and says something like, "Well, that about covers it," that is your cue to ask the commitment question: "Would you like better results than you're currently getting with everyone in the department, starting today?" The answer to this question is what determines whether the conversation continues to a resolution—that is, gets the green light—or gets the red light and ends the conversation. Pre-Emptive Leaders who focus on letting people solve their own situations should target this commitment question.

Solution Focus: If you've gotten the green light, you and your team member will now be able to put together possible solutions and focus on actions that each of you can take. When you get to this step, start with the employee and focus on positive steps that he can take, reminding him of all the possibilities that are open to him. At this point, your conversation has really become powerful, as you've allowed it to transition forward. You have taken the energy of frustration and redirected it to moving ahead.

Action Plan: From this conversation, you and your employee can create a plan for what each of you is going to do. "I really need to adjust my tone of voice," he might say, to which you might reply, "And I need to be more open with you." Your employee may admit that he needs to share more information about projects with others who are involved and, in return, you can suggest regular meetings to discuss team priorities. Together, you can come up with a multitude of ways in which you can improve the tense situation that brought you together in the first place, and these ideas are the basis of an action plan.

Acknowledge: You and your team member must agree that no matter what happens after this discussion, you will give each other feedback on how it's going. Many managers fail to communicate in this way when there's tension; unfortunately, they also fail to communicate when there's progress. Relying on each other to give feedback and follow-up on action plans will sustain productive behaviors for the long run.

Facilitated Conversation Checklist

EVALUATE: FACILITATOR PREPARATION
_____ 1. Is tension or miscommunication affecting productivity?
_____ 2. Are policies being adhered to?
_____ 3. Have the parties casually tried to resolve this situation?
_____ 4. Is the timing right?
_____ 5. Will conflict resolution be supported by the manager(s)?
_____ 6. Am I a neutral facilitator?

GO DIRECT & IN THE OPEN: TELL ME ABOUT IT
_____ 1. Communicate "Conversation Map" agenda.
_____ 2. Observation Statement: open with one behavior
"I've noticed..." or "I understand..."
_____ 3. Program people to talk; communication is a 50/50 dialogue. Write down topics of venting/storming to track repeated subjects.
_____ 4. Listen, ask clarifying questions. DO NOT FIX IT!

SOLUTIONS & ACTION PLAN: GET THE SCORE
_____ 1. Commitment Question — determines red or green light.
"Would you like different results than we currently have regarding _____ starting today?"
_____ 2. If you get a **red light** — communicate the situation will not be resolved on the front wheel. That is OK, it is their choice.
_____ 3. If you get a **green light** — the situation moves to action plan.
"What is one action you will implement starting TODAY?"
_____ 4. Action plans must be written. Each person receives a copy before they leave the meeting.

ACKNOWLEDGE: FEEDBACK PROCESS
_____ 1. Positive feedback reinforces action plan. _PROVIDE IMMEDIATELY._
_____ 2. Negative feedback reinforces action plan. _PROVIDE IMMEDIATELY._
"Go to each other first if you perceive an action plan is not being acted upon." Communicate: **"I'm confused, my understanding of the actions were..."**
_____ 3. One chance to slip from action plan.
_____ 4. People choose to be a part of the team/solution or not.
"Contact me together if the commitments are not being implemented. From today on, our discussions will only be on the action plans."

ACKNOWLEDGE: FOLLOW-UP
_____ 1. Schedule follow-up session or phone call prior to completing session.
_____ 2. Follow-up session reviews progress of action plan.
_____ 3. Add additional action plans only if tension still exists.

Facilitated Conversation

In each red light/green light scenario, your employee will need to answer the commitment question. Of course, it would be ideal for him to give you the green light, so that you can then go on to solve the conflict together.

But sometimes that's just not the case. When you do approach an employee with an issue that needs to be discussed, keep in mind that there is always the chance that he or she will be taken off guard, and will become upset by what you have to say and give you the "red light" instead. This is okay; there's no need for you to get emotional about it. At that point, you can simply say to your team member, "At this point, we're stuck. I had hoped you would like to solve this together, but we do have other options. We could ask someone to facilitate a conversation between you and me and the other team members—perhaps even another manager. What would you like to do?"

If your employee truly wants to work through this conflict, he will agree to the facilitated conversation, and your letting him have the choice of facilitator really gives him a feeling of having a stake in the issue's outcome, since he will be able to select someone he knows and trusts. Whether or not the facilitator is familiar with the details of the conflict is not essential; the facilitator is there not to solve the conflict but to guide you, your employee and any other involved team members to solve it yourselves.

The facilitator can be anyone who is familiar with the Conversation Map's steps (see Facilitated Conversation Checklist). An example of conflict resolution through a facilitated conversation is outlined in the following scenario:

Evaluate: The first step on the Conversation Map calls for the facilitator to make sure that he's using the right tools to solve the conflict, and that the process will be supported by all team members involved. The facilitator ascertains that the timing is right for everyone and that the Conversation Map is the right tool for this specific conflict. If members do not support using the map for conflict resolution, the conflict transitions to the back wheel where management decides how to resolve the conflict for the team members involved.

Go Direct: Using the checklist (see Facilitated Conversation graphic), the facilitator opens with an observation statement such as, "I understand that there is tension existing within the team. Let's talk about it."

In the Open: Over a period of twenty minutes, each participant in this meeting gets an opportunity to STORM while everyone else listens without interrupting. For example, if there are four people in the meeting, each person updates the others for up to five minutes or until they start repeating themselves. The facilitator's role here is to foster an environment in which team members feel safe to open up and talk—not to fix or solve the conflict. The faster-paced communicators will most likely speak up first; the facilitator should let them have their say, and then call on those who haven't spoken and ask for their input. This gives each person a chance to express an opinion, and gives everyone good practice in both communicating and listening.

Red Light/Green Light: The facilitator should now ask each person the commitment question, one by one: "Would you like different results for this situation, starting today?" For those who opt for the green light—the "yes" choice—the facilitator can help them move on to the FORM portion of the learning curve by asking them, "What could you do starting today to make a difference?" Employees who choose the red light—those who choose "no"—are merely expressing that they are not ready to solve the situation themselves at this time. This is an acceptable answer; however, all members must communicate green lights to continue using the Conversation Map as a resolution tool. As stated earlier, if all members are not ready to solve the situation, the map is no longer used and the conflict transitions over to the back wheel where management decides how to resolve the conflict for the team members involved.

Solution Focus: If all parties give a green light, then you move into *solution focus* and discuss the ways in which each of them will take the responsibility to move the situation forward. This is where team members start to get excited; because they've been allowed to get emotions off their chests, they feel free to come up with numerous ideas. They are ready for change, and do not want to talk about what's not working anymore. They want to move on. This step closes the gap of miscommunication and empowers each team member with the responsibility of resolving the situation; just keep in mind that some individuals move to *solution focus* sooner than others, and it is important that the facilitator not rush those who take a little longer.

Action Plan: At this point, each participant will be asked to come up with an action plan—something that they will do, starting today, to reduce the tension. For example, one will choose to attend a staff meeting every week to present his ideas on the current project; another will meet with the first employee prior to the meetings, so that they can consolidate their thoughts; still others may resolve to change their attitudes by going direct to their fellow team members whenever they experiences confusion or misunderstanding. As the leader, you can agree to make yourself more available by meeting with your team members at a particular time every week.

Acknowledge: In this last step of the Conversation Map, team members agree to communicate better with each other about what is and is not working, and to acknowledge each other's achievements or lack of commitment to the action plan in order to encourage each other toward success. As the facilitator, before the meeting adjourns schedule a follow-up session to be held within two weeks. The purpose of the follow-up session is to celebrate progress—not to see if participants kept their commitments. Participants will acknowledge each other immediately and directly if, by chance, commitments are not being kept.

Taking the Back Wheel Option

Sometimes, when a front wheel issue is affecting productivity, an employee will choose to have a manager resolve the issue at hand, rather than participate in a facilitated conversation. This is the "red light" option of the map. In this case, a team member can go to a manager and talk to him about the conflict and about the tension it's been causing in the workplace. Then, the team member can ask the manager to clarify how the issue should be resolved. In this scenario, the manager makes the decision and communicates his expectations as to what members in conflict must do to resolve the situation without using the Conversation Map.

In our training, managers will sometimes ask us why they can't just start with this step—that is, why they can't just go to the manager and resolve the conflict using the back wheel approach and get the whole thing done quickly. Our answer, of course, is always the same: because this is not a long-term solution. Though it's useful and appropriate to be told what to do in some situations, in general people like and should be encouraged to think for themselves. And the majority of the time, when employees are allowed to resolve their own conflicts, they do so effectively—and the solutions they implement will last.

Avoiding Attack-Defend Conflict

Although conflict is an essential problem-solving tool, it should not be approached as an attack-defend interaction. Telling team members what to do doesn't get long-term results. We need a different, front wheel tool. Pre-Emptive Leaders are trusted coaches who teach team members to speak up, listen to one another and solve their own problems.

To illustrate this phenomenon, we'll use an example from the personal side of life. Suppose you go home at night and discover that your teenager wrecked the family car. You would probably demand to know what happened, but when your child tries to explain what may have been a faultless accident, you would go on the defensive, blaming your child for what happened and telling her that she should not have been speeding, should have been more careful, or whatever admonishment fits.

This is an example of an attack-defend conflict, wherein the speaker attacks someone who has done something offensive to them, and then tries to defend their outburst by putting blame on the other party. Attack-defend is always an unproductive method of conversation and should be avoided as much as possible—both at home and at work.

Instead, try using the conversation map to work your way through this situation. Allow your son or daughter a ten-minute STORM phase to explain what happened; let them talk until they repeat themselves, and make sure that you listen carefully. Then, take your own ten minutes to speak your thoughts as your son or daughter listens. At the end of the STORM period, ask each other, "Would we like different results than we currently have?" Hopefully, you will both indicate "yes," and give the green light. Then, you can ask each other, "What could we do, starting right now, to make this situation better?"

When you're stuck in the attack-defend mode, you can be so busy reacting that you don't take the valuable opportunity to teach your child how to communicate and how to listen. By utilizing the Conversation Map, whether you're dealing with problems at home or at work, you can facilitate a tough conversation anywhere, with anyone, very effectively.

Pre-Emptive Leaders address front wheel situations affecting productivity with the same urgency as back wheel situations. The goal is to spend more time on possible solutions and very little time on who did what to whom; blame does not matter, and attacking is never the right thing to do. The point is to get to a solution that will last.

There is no reason that a conversation should ever be unproductive if you use the Conversation Map and the other Pre-Emptive tools you're learning about in this book. Remember that you do not always have to be the problem solver or mediator; all you need to do is follow the steps of the map, and encourage your employees to do the same.

Common Shortcuts

One of the best suggestions we can make to our clients who are learning how to be leaders within their organizations, whatever their communication style, is to never take shortcuts. Never skip over a step

Resolve Misunderstandings Now 59

in the Conversation Map. Don't repeat steps, either—don't go back and rehash what you've already covered; this does nothing but give people more negative things to think about instead of moving forward toward resolution.

Shortcuts can be a major problem, though, when you're trying to push for results. Does this look like any conversations you've had with your employees lately?

> **Manager:** I've noticed that you haven't been acting as though you're part of the team lately, and I'm wondering what your thoughts are on that.
> **Employee:** I agree. There's a problem.
> **Manager:** Here's what we can we do to fix it.

If this sounds like the way you communicate, it means that you're a faster-paced, back wheel communicator, and you may not be getting the results that you're after. The reason for this? Your conversation is incomplete—you have taken a shortcut to the STORM phase, and have not let your team members get things off their chests and determine if THEY want to solve the situation or not. You have become too focused on your *action plan*, have not heard their thoughts on the subject, and did not get their buy-in—without which they will not follow through on the solution you came up with. When managers get excited about employees acknowledging a problem, they can get into trouble because they fail to ask for the employees' commitment. Without the commitment, the problem will continue.

If, instead, you're more of a faster-paced, front wheel communicator, you may tend to shortcut the *evaluate* stage and head right for the STORM phase of the learning curve. Since you're using your leadership skills and going directly to your employees, you may think that it's a good idea to go up to a team member who's having some problems and say, "Do you know what people are saying about you? When you were at lunch, they said that you hadn't completed a report."

But this is really not the way to go. This is putting your own STORM onto the employee, instead of letting him figure things out for himself; it's called "stirring the pot," and it's a telltale habit of a reactive manager, not a Pre-Emptive Leader.

Conversely, slower-paced, front wheel communicators tend to stay in *evaluate* mode forever—and in fact never even get around to having the conversation with the employee. They think about it, and know that they should do it, but it just never happens, whether from fear or lack of time or whatever excuse the manager wants to give. This can create so much tension in the workplace—on the part of the manager, who lives with that phantom conversation hanging over his head, and on the part of the employee, whose needs are never addressed—but everyone lives with it because they don't trust each other enough to confront the situation.

Slower-paced, back wheel communicators have their own short-cuts as well. They usually go straight to the *solution focus* instead of finding the right balance between evaluation, going directly to the employee and allowing them to STORM.

In this scenario, the manager takes an investigative approach and tries to find out if anyone else has a problem with the employee in question. This is appropriate if a back wheel procedure or policy, such as harassment or discrimination, has been broken, but if you're dealing with front wheel issues involving only the employee and no one else, an investigation is inappropriate. When this is the case, the only person who needs to know about it—and the only one who can fix it—is the employee, and he can't do that if he's not aware of the problem.

In a Nutshell

Pre-Emptive Leaders encourage conflict rather than run away from it. They understand that productive conflict is necessary for advancement and growth. By investing the time upfront to create a team that can sustain itself, Pre-Emptive Leaders set their employees up for success because they will be better equipped to deal with conflict when it arises.

The Conversation Map is an effective Pre-Emptive Leadership tool for facilitating difficult conversations. By following its steps—evaluate, go direct, in the open, red light/green light, solution focus, action plan

Resolve Misunderstandings Now **61**

and acknowledge—leaders can resolve conflicts between employees and themselves, and build an important foundation of trust with the members of the team.

While utilizing the Conversation Map, leaders may find that facilitation is necessary in order to resolve the conflict. Employing the help of an employee-chosen facilitator can help move the conversation along productively; so can allowing the manager to step in and solve the problem for others, although this is not a preferred first method of action.

When confronted by an employee with a problem, it's important not to go into attack-defend mode, wherein we attack the person with the issue and then become defensive when they try to explain. This is unproductive; try following the Conversation Map instead.

It's common to take shortcuts that can derail the Conversation Map's effectiveness. Make sure that when utilizing the map, you complete all the steps, in order, to solve the conflict and achieve the results that you want.

What's Next?

Motivation directly relates to personal-need satisfaction and it's important for Pre-Emptive Leaders to understand what makes people "tick." In the next chapter, we'll look at the fourth step in the Pre-Emptive Leadership System, which involves understanding what causes a team member to take action and strive toward success.

CHAPTER 4

Know What Makes a Person Tick

If you've been practicing the first three steps of Pre-Emptive Leadership on a regular basis, you should be getting better results in the workplace than you ever have before. Your relationships with your employees should be improving as you build a foundation of trust with them, which shows in their increased productivity.

Perhaps, however, there are still some people on your team whom you haven't been able to reach. They are still adversely affecting productivity, and a clear solution to this issue has not yet presented itself to you. You're certain that you don't have a communication problem with these people, and you've resolved any conflict or misunderstandings that there may have been, but they're just not responding.

Consider Motivation

Before you chalk the problem up to these employees just "not getting it," consider their motivation. Though most of us expect our coworkers to be as motivated as we are, that's rarely the rule; all people are motivated differently and find different reasons to work toward success—or not, if their motivation is low.

If you want the members of your team to consistently do what you ask them to, you need to understand what motivates each one—and it has to be more than just a desire to please you, their leader. Motivation is the perfect blend of a team member's drive and the actions he performs; if the former outweighs the latter, you have a motivated individual, one who exceeds what is expected of him because of his enthusiasm for the work. If, on the other hand, the actions needed are greater than the drive, you have an unmotivated individual—one who works on the required tasks but seems disinterested or apathetic toward them.

In one of our training exercises, we ask participants to raise their right hands. Then we ask, "Why did you do that?"

Most of the responses are along the lines of, "Because you told us to."

Next, we tell everyone to get up, put their chairs on their backs and run around the building five times. Needless to say, this command is met with some confused looks, even some laughter. Why is this? Why are most people unwilling to perform more difficult tasks on demand?

The reason is that raising a hand is a small action with no motive other than pleasing the person who requests that you do it. Our training participants raised their hands because it required little effort, but don't expect people to do what you ask just because you ask them to do it.

Your employees' motivation to perform requested tasks depends upon the level of motivation involved. The clearer the motive, the more quickly they will complete the action; the larger the action you want them to perform, the clearer the motive must be. When it comes to complex or difficult tasks, you need to provide motivation for your team members in order to get them to do it.

Here's an example. Another question we ask in our training is, "If someone asks you to run around the building five times for two thousand dollars, would you do it?" This isn't even a demand on our part, yet whenever we say it, several people always get up from their chairs

Know What Makes a Person Tick

as if they're going to run toward the door! What would motivate someone to perform this higher-level action—one that requires much more effort on their part? Obviously, it's the larger payoff. Far from just the innate satisfaction of feeling as though we've pleased the "teacher," the promise of a good monetary reward is quite motivating to some.

As a Pre-Emptive Leader, this is the sort of distinction that you need to make: You must know what motivates people—each of them individually—in order to influence their actions. When you can look at each of your team members and figure out what would motivate each of them to do the best job they possibly can, and then offer that to them, they will work harder for you than you ever would have expected.

> *You must know what motivates people—each of them individually—in order to influence their actions*

Reactive managers don't think about what makes team members tick like this. Instead, they fall into that trap of just expecting everyone else to do their jobs for the same reason they do: because they have to, and because they're afraid not to. It's not uncommon for a reactive manager to ask, "Why should I have to come up with a motive or a reason? I pay these people. They should just do what they're supposed to."

Reactive managers mistakenly believe that because they tell team members to do something, they should do it. We've seen that although this may work for small tasks that require little investment on the employees' part, when it comes to higher-level actions, the employees are not likely to comply.

Three Motivational Factors

There are three common factors that motivate people to perform to their highest potential: appreciation, involvement and awareness of personal situations. Pre-Emptive Leaders know how to use these factors to motivate team members to *want* to do what needs to be done.

Many reactive managers are surprised to discover that money is not one of these three top motivational factors. Motivation in the workplace

66   **It All Starts With YOU**

is often linked to money, and with good reason; getting a paycheck is one of the main reasons people go to work in the first place. But as far as a reason for completing tasks, it's not very high on the list.

Even if you inherit a new team from a reactive manager and you know nothing about the people you'll be leading, you can tailor these three factors so they will motivate the entire team, individually and as a group, and utilize them to impact every member of your team in a positive way. This is how Pre-Emptive Leaders create sustainable, high-performing teams.

Now, let's take a look at the three motivational factors in more depth.

Appreciation

Though it's the most powerful of the three factors, appreciation must be used appropriately; that old saying about "too much of a good thing" definitely applies here. If an employee hears how great he is doing every day—no matter what quality of work he's turning out—this appreciation becomes meaningless to him, and comes across as a fake managerial tactic to coerce him to get the work done.

Pre-Emptive Leaders, on the other hand, know well enough to show appreciation only when it is fully warranted, and are careful to recognize team members in ways that work for them individually. Words of praise don't work for everyone; in fact, they can turn some people off. The trick here is to know what each person will respond to, and make sure that they get it.

Let's go back to our bicycle analogy to see how, as a leader, you can utilize appreciation most effectively in correlation with communication *priorities*:

- **Back wheel** communicators need recognition to be very tangible, in the forms of accomplishments, tasks completed or goals achieved.

- **Front wheel** communicators need recognition to be intangible—that is, touchy-feely, emotional and expressive.

Know What Makes a Person Tick 67

Now, let's add in communication *pace*:

- **Faster-paced** communicators like public appreciation; they like to openly communicate with others about what they've accomplished.

- **Slower-paced** communicators are motivated by private appreciation. This means communicating one-on-one or via e-mail—in a setting where accomplishments are not openly announced.

And finally, we can put *priority* and *pace* together to come up with a full picture of the different approaches you might take in order to most effectively reach your team members:

- **Faster-paced, back wheel** communicators are motivated by public, tangible appreciation. These team members tend to have large houses and luxury cars; their offices commonly have the walls full of plaques and awards. Publicly given, tangible signs of appreciation keep them motivated because they like having something that they—and others—can see.

- **Faster-paced, front wheel** communicators are motivated by one-minute praise sessions. Intangible terms like "wonderful work," "fabulous improvement" and "outstanding job" motivate these team members, who are likely to not only show you their letters of praise from clients, but ask you to read them aloud, and to post them on the department bulletin board as well.

- **Slower-paced, front wheel** communicators prefer their appreciation to be more private; to them, public praise is an instant turn off. Meet with these team members one-on-one to communicate with them, and use phrases such as "the team" and "the contributions your team has made." If time does not allow a personal meeting, leave a card or sticky note on their desk to acknowledge their efforts—they'll save them and, when they need a burst of energy, pull them out and re-read them.

- **Slower-paced, back wheel** communicators are motivated by GOMB: *Get off my back.* "Employee appreciation days" are like punishment to them; you'll rarely see them at a company picnic unless attendance is mandatory. These employees say, "Don't tell me I'm wonderful. Just let me do my job." Giving them responsibility in conjunction with authority creates a high level of motivation; this form of recognition communicates that you trust their expertise.

Involvement

Part of being an excellent leader is being aware of how change affects the people with whom you work. Any time you have a change in the organization—hirings, firings, schedule shifts and so on—ask yourself which people in your department will be affected by it and then send them some quick e-mails to prepare them for the change and pre-empt any problems that it may cause. For example, you could e-mail them a message such as, "We are restructuring the office. Here's what we are planning… If you have any questions, come see me." Letting them know that you are available to them—and that it is alright for them to STORM over these changes—can create a high level of motivation simply because it shows your team members that you care about their satisfaction and security.

Unfortunately, most reactive managers do not consider their employees when changes are impending within the organization. They may share information with team members who happen to be around at the time, but fail to think about how those who they do not include will feel about being "left out." Such a lack of information sharing is viewed as disrespectful—especially when employees come in to work one day and find that their desks have been moved, their workday lengthened or their coworkers laid off. This shows them that their manager is not trustworthy and has no psychological commitment to the team members. When needs such as these are

Know What Makes a Person Tick

not met, team members do not feel valued and therefore are not motivated.

Awareness

Having a high awareness of team members' personal situations is a great way to create motivation in the workplace. If the people on your team trust you enough to open up and tell you about what is going on in their lives, chances are they will feel a connection to you—which in turn will make them more agreeable and driven when it comes to the work they have to do.

Reactive managers who are more focused on back wheel tasks tend to distance themselves from their team members' personal situations and feel, in general, that employees should leave their personal lives at home. Conversely, managers who are more focused on front wheel issues can get *too* wrapped up in team members' problems and have trouble separating the "drama" from their managerial responsibilities. Neither of these is a good situation to be in.

Take a look at the team members you view as difficult—the ones from whom you are not getting the results you desire. Do you know the names and ages of their kids? Do you know what they'd do right now with an extra thousand dollars in their checking account, or where they would go on a two-week vacation? What are their greatest fears and their greatest sources of pride? Their hobbies?

It's not uncommon for managers to be unaware of such things when it comes to their employees but, as a leader, you have to make these details your business. If you want people to produce at the level you need them to, you have to know what they value, and what they enjoy doing. You have to create that common bond, that trust, in order to motivate them toward success.

This is rarely a problem, however, for Pre-Emptive Leaders, who are naturally tuned in to what their team members are saying. If an employee is late because his mother is sick, a Pre-Emptive Leader will not be annoyed, as a reactive manager would be; instead, he would ask the employee, "How's your mom doing?" Then he will listen to whatever his team member wants to say, without giving advice or being nosy.

70　　　　It All Starts With YOU

The bottom line is engagement—that is the top motivator that a leader can work with, not money or other tangible rewards. When leaders engage their employees based on the employees' own interests and show them how much they are valued for their talents, the employees will be motivated to excel.

External Motivation

Once you start properly motivating your team, you will find that looking into what makes its members "tick" is well worth your time—but it does take a little insight and investigation. First, you have to understand that people in general do things for one of two reasons: to avoid a loss, or to gain a benefit. While one person is motivated to act by his desire to avoid a particular consequence (a loss), another's motivation comes from his drive to work

> *You have to understand that people in general do things for one of two reasons: to avoid a loss, or to gain a benefit*

toward some sort of goal (a benefit). These two schools of thought are referred to as external motivation based on fear and incentive, and they have been around for quite a long time.

Now, take a minute and think about which of these best describes you. Do you act more on the basis of avoiding a potential loss? Or is your main concern the benefit you will gain at the end of the job? It's possible for the answer to be both, and that's one thing you need to keep in mind while trying to motivate your employees: Some will respond better to fear and others to incentive. Some will respond to a mixture of the two.

When an employee is motivated by fear, she is dead-set on proving everyone else wrong—especially if the others are saying that she cannot do the task, that she will fail in her endeavor or not succeed with her plans. Someone whose life runs on this method is motivated by a potential loss. When her alarm clock rings in the morning, she asks herself, "What will happen if I don't show up for work today?" Her desire is to avoid the consequence of not going to work; that's what gets her out of bed and into action—the motivation to avoid whatever penalty might come from skipping work.

Know What Makes a Person Tick

Fear is the most common type of motivation used in the workplace. Threats, looming consequences and the possibility of job loss are all the tools of this method and provide motivation for employees to keep doing their jobs. Though this may not be thought of as a form of motivation, it is one that works if the person to be motivated thrives on avoiding a potential loss. If you want to understand how it works, ask yourself why people drive under the speed limit and pay their taxes.

Reactive managers are sometimes guilty of overusing (and even abusing) this fear of loss motivation; unable to discern who will respond to it best, they instead try to instill fear in all of the employees across the board.

Pre-Emptive Leaders, on the other hand, are able to figure out which of their team members respond well to this type of motivation and use it as a method to help them work to their fullest potential. Of course, they do this in a productive manner; instead of threatening jobs or demeaning the team members personally, leaders use fear-of-loss statements such as "I'm not sure you can handle it" and "This may not be for you," knowing that employees who respond best to fear will be motivated by the desire to prove them wrong.

Employees who are motivated by incentive approach things entirely differently. When their alarm rings in the morning, they're already thinking about how they will be rewarded for showing up at work. This can be largely due to Pre-Emptive Leaders, who understand the value of providing motivation to such people on a daily basis by talking about goals and achievements, dreams and visions, and next steps that these team members can take to further their work or their careers.

Some reactive managers try to interact with incentive-driven team members in this way, but often take the topic to extremes. They may say things such as, "You'll get a promotion," "You'll get a raise" or "Perhaps we might look at a new job for you down the road" on a regular basis—which is too often.

Such seemingly motivational statements are of limited appeal to Pre-Emptive Leaders, who prefer a more realistic approach. They use positive statements with employees who derive the most from benefit-centered motivation, but frame them in such a way as to make them attainable—such as, "Here's what we'll gain," "This is where we're heading" and "If we accomplish this, we'll get new clients, more business, or be viewed as experts."

Internal Motivation

When we lead sessions on motivation, almost all people in the audience state that they are internally motivated—that is, they can motivate themselves to do a good job without incentives or fear. The problem is that these people are not as common as the loss and benefit people, and most people in our training who claim to be internally motivated discover that they really aren't.

Employees tend to think that if they're not internally motivated, others—especially managers—will think there's something wrong with them. Many people are truly internally motivated and operate as such, but many more are simply trying to pass themselves off as the same, simply because they think it's the image they're supposed to project.

Everyone is internally motivated to some extent about something in life—but, unfortunately, this condition is very selective. You only have to look so far as your teenage son or daughter to understand this: Ask them to mow the lawn or clean their room and they'll be too tired, but as soon as a friend calls with an invitation to go out, they're suddenly full of energy. They were internally motivated by something there, but it certainly wasn't the household chores.

When it comes to the workplace, internally motivated team members are the ones who know how to make their motives bigger than their actions. They are very clear about what their active needs are and about what makes them tick, and they have aligned those needs with what they do for a living so that there's a level of connection between the needs and the job.

The Approach

Pre-Emptive Leaders motivate team members by conversing with them on a daily basis, using a combination of different types of motivation. Most sales teams use incentive/reward—and only incentive/reward—

Know What Makes a Person Tick 73

and so end up having the same team members outperforming everyone else month after month. It is great that these star players are so motivated and successful, but it's obvious that everyone else is lagging behind because the managers fail to use a mixture of motivational methods to inspire everyone.

In another example, a company might have a sales manager who uses only fear as a motivator. As a result, only a portion of the team is motivated, and a small portion at that; statistics show that if you have six members on your team, two will be motivated by fear, two by incentive/reward and two by their own internal motivation. Addressing only one of these—and, generally, it's the one that works for the manager himself—is the downfall of many a reactive manager's production levels. This is the complete opposite of Pre-Emptive Leaders, who use all three motivational methods in order to hit a maximum productivity level.

Motivational Needs

Most people haven't thought about what motivates them. They reach a burnout level and don't understand why. Only after understanding the different types and factors of motivation, and how those methods relate to their individual needs, do they gain insight into how to motivate themselves as well as setting the stage to motivate others.

After studying the needs below, try to figure out the top two needs for the team members you want to motivate—and for yourself. These needs will vary based on the situations and experiences the person is going through at a particular moment in their life.

An interesting discovery from working with leaders for over twenty years is that they tend to work against their primary motivational needs when trying to fulfill them. What you really need to do, as a leader, is work *with* your needs and motivate yourself as well as others to work to your full potential. If you're not going to set an example of motivation, you won't be able to influence people to attain their greatest level of performance.

All of our needs are important and valuable—there is no such thing as a best need. Below, we've come up with a partial list of needs

74　　　　　　　　**It All Starts With YOU**

that leaders as well as team members may have. See which ones you relate to the most, and see how you can pique your own level of motivation toward these needs in the next two weeks. We have also provided suggestions for how to proceed toward that goal.

- **A Need for Accomplishment.** If you have this, you want to see that you're making progress in order to build momentum and get things done. However, if this is one of your top two needs, you're probably doing the opposite—you're constantly working against the need by thinking about all of the things you haven't accomplished. Try thinking instead about all the things that have gone right, and stop focusing so much on what's left to do. Enjoy the ride, and avoid inner conflict that results in burnout and not operating at your peak level.
  In the next two weeks: Make a list of everything you've accomplished. Modify your to-do list into an achievement list.

- **A Need to Create.** This need is expressed by your desire to come up with solutions outside of your regular day-to-day activities. You find it very motivating to be asked to be part of a project team—and to go in knowing nothing, but to still be able to offer solutions. If you're working against this need, you're not venturing outside your comfort level, which might be encouraged by a reactive manager who tells you things such as, "Just worry about your own area." Staying in your own work area, however, can make you feel underutilized, and can give others the impression that you are not someone who should be listened to. The key is to take action—to initiate it yourself, and then venture outside of your own function.
  In the next two weeks: Pursue projects and teams outside your work area. Actively participate in staff meetings, retreats and special projects.

- **A Need to Lead.** You want to be able to influence teams, and you want more of the spotlight. Being in charge and taking

Know What Makes a Person Tick 75

ownership of projects motivates you, and you are first to step up in meetings and start facilitating. Even as part of a team, you can feel this need; however, if it's stifled, you can become controlling, overpowering and aggressive. Even those who are not formal leaders must be allowed to practice some kind of informal leadership, or they may become disgruntled and leave the business.

In the next two weeks: Meet with your manager about ideas you feel should be pursued and set up opportunities to informally lead. Volunteer to take on more responsibility and projects.

- **A Need to be Informed.** Being in the loop and knowing what's going on behind the scenes is extremely motivating for you. What really shuts you down is coming in to discover that changes have occurred even though you were not asked for input or told about them in advance. When this need is not met, you burn out; you work against this need by not asking for clarification and not taking initiative.

  In the next two weeks: Determine what you need to know about and ask questions that will get you the information. Get yourself on a distribution list of key topics that are pertinent to your job.

- **A Need for Advancement.** Team members who are motivated to take on additional responsibilities can bring huge dividends for an organization. Typically, a company will respond to this situation by taking the best-performing candidates and making them managers. This is a huge mistake—especially in sales, where the best performers are seldom the best managers. Those who are technically the best are often intense doers who are always in their offices; people are generally not attracted to them. The technical best need to be motivating, and they need to have team members want to follow them.

If you think that there's no way for you to advance in the organization, you're working against this need. Instead, ask yourself what type of front wheel skills you can use to get ahead. Do you need to work on your patience or other skills? What back wheel skills do you need? Working on this plan will keep your motivation up.

In the next two weeks: Meet with your manager. Talk about a specific leadership path, as well as a career-development plan. Discuss additional education. What skills need development? What books should you read?

- **A Need for Independence.** "Think time" is one of your major needs. You are constantly around others and if you don't get a chance to recharge, you will reach a high level of burnout. You can't be forced to train others; instead of being required to work with others, you prefer self-starter projects such as writing a training manual or standard operating procedure.

  In the next two weeks: Take at least thirty minutes a day for think time, planning time, or just reading a book.

- **A Need to Interact.** Those who are motivated by interaction are usually lacking it. This need often occurs when you're in an inner office or working from home. Because of your high affiliation need, if you're isolated, you aren't motivated to work. When this need is not met, you are not focused—you're distracted and not at peak, seem to be wasting time and don't get much done. This is because you lack the motive to create the required action.

  Many companies will put a senior leader in a corner office. This could be a big mistake. The isolated leader will grab a cup of coffee, mill around and chitchat. If you put the work area in a cube in the middle of the office, the need will be met, the Corner Office Syndrome will vanish, and the senior leader will be more productive than ever before.

Know What Makes a Person Tick
77

In the next two weeks: Set up interaction activities, such as conference calls, virtual meetings or team-related projects. Give yourself social outlets.

- **A Need for Incentive.** In order to be motivated, you need a clear-cut "carrot"—a determined goal. If you pay off your credit cards, your motivation goes down because you don't have the next goal to achieve. Buying a new car or any other tangible goal motivates you; if you aren't acquiring something, you get uncomfortable and burn out. When working against this need, you can become comfortably numb, and start leaving work early on a regular basis to go to dinner or take weekend vacations.
  It's imperative that you know where you're headed when this is your need. You need a focused awareness of what the next event is. Crystallize your thoughts and bring your goal more into focus by asking organizational questions such as, "What goal do I want to attain next?" Perhaps the answer will be, "I want to go on a cruise." The object here is to converse about an event that you can visualize and plan for.
  In the next two weeks: Get out a calendar and do some goal setting—plan your next vacation or acquisition, so that it's really clear why you're getting out of bed in the morning.

- **A Need to Help.** If you're motivated by volunteering and serving others, you have a need to feel that you can share your talents. Sometimes, you may even create a problem so you can solve it! If this need isn't being met, you can find yourself helping with too many things, and spreading yourself too thin. When you have too much going on, you can't really make a difference, which is the one need that drives you.
  In the next two weeks: Narrow down where you can really make a difference. Drop all of your committees and really hone in on the one area where you can see the results of your talents and energies.

- **A Need for Appreciation.** As you've already learned, everyone is motivated by appreciation, but those who have it as a top need should recognize and appreciate themselves first. If this is one of your top needs, you often work against it by waiting for someone else to praise you. Part of the problem might be your communication style. If you are a faster-paced, back wheel communicator, you need public, tangible results. If you're faster-paced front wheel, you need public, intangible recognition. As a slower-paced, front wheel type, you will prefer private, intangible recognition. If you're a slower-paced, back wheel communicator, you'll need private, tangible recognition. **In the next two weeks:** Based upon your style of communication, provide yourself with daily recognition of the type that you prefer. Appreciate yourself by providing incremental rewards every day. Waiting for someone else to appreciate you is not the answer.

In a Nutshell

Everyone is motivated differently and, as a leader, it is important for you to figure out what each of your team members responds to best, and use that to help them achieve more than they've ever been able to before. By utilizing the three motivational factors—appreciation, involvement and awareness of personal situations—you can create a strong bond of trust with your employees and motivate them to work to their full potential.

People who are externally motivated rely upon one of two methods for their motivation: fear of loss or the prospect of an incentive or benefit. The former react to challenges from their leaders the best and strive to prove negative statements about them wrong; the latter look forward to what they will gain from an activity, be it a tangible reward such as money or an intangible "Job well done!" accolade.

In order to motivate your team members, you must first figure out what motivates you. Examine your motivational needs and make a plan for what you can do to motivate yourself in the next two weeks, then act on that plan to see the results you desire.

What's Next?

When the team's productivity is not meeting expectations or requirements, reactive managers become stressed out and blame it all on their employees without examining the role they play in the breakdown. In the next chapter, we'll see how Pre-Emptive Leaders provide clear, direct and honest communication with team members about what is expected of them—and positive, productive role models of "what right looks like."

CHAPTER 5
What Right Looks Like: Clarifying Expectations

When performance is declining, it's important to look not only at what you can do to fix it, but *why* it is going downhill in the first place. This is a step that reactive managers often skip, tending instead to just give in to the stress and complain that "people don't work the way they used to."

Part of the problem here is that team members need to know what is expected of them—but often do not get this clarification. Why is it so difficult for managers to come out and say what they expect from their team members? Fear of confrontation has something to do with it; so does a lack of trust and accountability.

Step five in the Pre-Emptive Leadership System involves remembering that people need clear, direct and honest communication of what right looks like; that is, they need to know what is expected of them in order to do their jobs well.

The Right Response

Back wheel skills are just as much a part of Pre-Emptive Leadership as front wheel skills—the challenge is in knowing when to use which. Sometimes, you have to let your employees think things through for themselves; other times, you just have to step in and tell them where things stand.

By solving their own issues, team members can grow to be empowered, autonomous individuals, which is one of the goals of Pre-Emptive Leadership. However, even with this sense of autonomy, there will be times when the team will just need to be told what to do, in order to move things along at the necessary pace.

Clarifying expectations is implementing management authority. There are two times when it is appropriate to use this tool: in front wheel situations when someone is not co-operating with the team, or when there is a misunderstanding about a back wheel policy or process. An example of the latter would be an employee not following accepted shipping procedures or a team member neglecting to implement a new policy.

Based on this, how would you deal with the following situation?

Tom, a member of the project team, is an average performer. His skills are not outstanding, but not poor. Recently, he's started arriving late for the team meetings that are held every Wednesday. Although he usually doesn't contribute much, his tardiness still affects the team. What would you do?

- Lay it on the line, and simply remind him that the meetings start promptly at 8:00.
- Change the meeting time to 8:30.
- When talking to Tom about other matters, mention to him that he needs to be more punctual.
- Compliment him when he does arrive close to the correct time.

If you've been operating in a reactive environment for a while, you may think that one or more of those options are acceptable. However, as a

What Right Looks Like: Clarifying Expectations   **83**

Pre-Emptive Leader, you will know that none of them will work long-term. The only effective solution to Tom's tardiness problem and average performance is to clarify the expectations you have for him by communicating in a positive, clear and direct manner what you expect of him, starting today. You could begin by saying to him, "Tom, starting today, there are three expectations that will be required to be in place," and then list them specifically for him. For example:

1. Be on time to all future 8:00 a.m. project meetings. Your punctuality is critical to the value of these meetings.
2. This week, meet with each member on the project team to find out how you can expedite the team's success. Find out from them what they expect and need from you in order to be a "real team."
3. Follow up with me next Friday with your top five actions for improving your performance with the project team, based on the feedback you received from your team members.

These expectations may sound obvious. However, they are rarely outwardly spoken by a reactive manager. Typically, a reactive manager just stays frustrated with Tom.

Let's look at another example: Suppose you have a presentation for a new customer due. You've had two weeks to complete it, and Jane, who is in charge of designing it, said it would be ready by Friday. That day comes and goes and, on Monday, Jane can't be reached and everybody's waiting.

This unproductive behavior has become a pattern with Jane, and a problem for the entire team. Other employees become frustrated when they have to rush to complete her work at the last minute; quality also suffers because what could have been well done with the right amount of time ends up being mediocre.

If you're the leader responsible for the team's results, you know exactly what to do about this situation with Jane. You already have a head start on it, actually, since you've been following the Pre-Emptive Leadership checklist:

- You have built a foundation of trust with your employees.
- You have made a connection with them.
- You have resolved misunderstandings.
- You have motivated your team members according to their individual needs.

Since Jane is a faster-paced, front wheel communicator, she will be motivated by incentive and though it may be a little late for her to redeem herself with the presentation project, you can pre-empt the same thing happening on her next assignment. When it's time to give her something new to work on, sit down with her and discuss the vision for the project and how she can contribute her own creative ideas to it. Give her a goal and a reward: Let her know that if the project is successful, you will make her the lead on one of the company's largest accounts.

This approach sounds great, but have you had this type of conversation before? If so, what's next?

The Clear Conversation

When you must meet with employees who have dropped the ball to clarify what is expected of them, the conversation should go something like this:

- First, say, "Starting today, this is what I expect from you."

- Second, note that all assignments must be completed by the agreed-upon deadline.

- Third, let them know that if an unexpected circumstance that may affect production arises, they must contact all other involved team members ahead of time so that the deadline can still be met.

- Fourth, tell them that they have to take responsibility for their own workload by prioritizing their projects or commitments

What Right Looks Like: Clarifying Expectations 85

and setting up work schedules that will allow them to meet their deadlines. This involves being realistic about what they can accomplish before agreeing to a completion date.

- Last, explain that they must take the initiative to ask questions of every team member involved when changes arise, rather than trying to tackle the problem by themselves. They work on a team, not alone, and they must remember and respect that.

At the end, after you have clarified all these expectations, remind your team members that these are not just expectations—they are requirements. Tell them, "These are not choices. They need to be implemented immediately. If you cannot fulfill these expectations, what do you think the next step should be?"

Asking this question will allow you to gauge your employees' commitment and ownership to meeting the expectations. When the expectations are spelled out clearly, people can decide for themselves whether or not their goals and those of the organization are a match, and what to do if this is the case. In our client companies, it's very rare for a Pre-Emptive Leader to have to terminate an employee, or even to engage in the first step of progressive discipline. This is a built-in function of the Pre-Emptive Leadership System: Those who cannot adhere to it will simply choose to "weed" themselves out.

It's very rare for a Pre-Emptive Leader to have to terminate an employee, or even to engage in the first step of progressive discipline

This approach is honest and specific. It tells your team members what right looks like and represents a very important tool because, quite often, they are *not* told exactly what is expected of them. They are familiar with reactive managers who merely say things such as, "Do what I hired you for," or, "Why can't you get it done when you say you can?" Reactive managers struggle with situations like these and often become frustrated, resorting to telling their employees, "If you don't meet deadlines that you've agreed to, there's going to be some disciplinary action." This makes them come across as weak because instead of clarifying, they resort to intimidation and threats.

Everyone has the right to know what's expected of them and as a leader, it is your job to communicate those expectations clearly. This requires using your back wheel skills and telling people what to do, and that's okay; this doesn't mean you're giving up on them or reverting to your old, reactive habits. In fact, when employees hear specifically what you want from them, it often feels like a breakthrough for team members who have never really been addressed with such clarity before.

The reactive manager's stand-offish approach to explaining expectations creates an atmosphere of confusion that can be difficult for employees to move out of. Perhaps the employees never even realized that they have the leeway to say that they're having trouble and cannot meet deadlines or demands. Maybe they've been allowed to miss deadlines before and don't realize that it's not okay to do so on a regular basis. Often, employees do not realize that they have the flexibility to ask other team members to help out when they get in a bind, or that they have the option to decline if they feel that they can't accomplish a project in a certain timeframe.

Reaching Out—No Matter How Hard It Is

The employees who are most difficult to approach are the eccentric ones, the extremely talented ones or the rainmakers who bring in the customer base. Reactive managers often mistakenly believe that such people are untouchable, and so do not go to them to clarify expectations. In turn, these team members question the manager's efficiency because the manager is obviously not addressing matters with them that need to be addressed.

This is not a situation that will improve with time but as a Pre-Emptive Leader, you can make the changes necessary to create a culture wherein these problems do not exist. You need to be a risk taker and act upon the principles you know are right. Team members will see this as being proactive and have a high level of respect for you.

What Right Looks Like: Clarifying Expectations 87

As a leader, you will know when to implement managerial authority and when to put more focus on "people issues." This balance of front wheel and back wheel skills rests on your ability to develop as a leader while sustaining high-performing teams.

For many organizations, however, this balance is difficult to achieve. Reactive managers get stuck; they let things go on too long by not addressing their organization's most glaring issues. They micromanage people with authority, using too much back wheel, and continually tell them what to do—but never really explain their expectations.

Pre-Emptive Leaders, on the other hand, will go back and forth between the front and back wheels over and over, balancing, pulling and pushing to ensure that they're using the right tools at the right times. Leaders use people skills when they communicate expectations, but at the same time they bring in that back wheel skill set as well. They let their employees know that when they, the leaders, make decisions, those are requirements that everyone must fulfill. For the most part, team members appreciate this. They want their leaders to take a stand.

Pre-Emptive Leaders walk a fine line between leading and managing, and must have the wisdom to decide when each is appropriate. Most often, they will let their teams try to manage themselves but when it becomes clear that the employees do not want to lead their own situations, the Pre-Emptive Leaders will manage things for them. They will step in and clarify expectations in a clear, informative, detailed and specific manner.

In such a situation, the leaders' responses are immediate, their intent to motivate and help. Even though they are using their back wheel skills and being more manager than leader for the time being, they can still allow team members to clarify things for themselves and provide their own input on the situation.

With this approach, there are no secrets, which alleviates the stress of having to discipline or even terminate an employee. When everything is upfront and transparent, and interactions align with the core values of teamwork, integrity and accountability, as we've mentioned before, those who do not fit in will weed themselves out. Those who

Reaping Your Own Rewards

With Pre-Emptive Leadership implemented in your organization, you will no longer lie awake at night, worrying about the latest problem at work or how you're going to get it all done. Instead, you'll sleep peacefully, knowing that the tools you have to work with as a leader will help you get ahead of the game. Your decisions at work will be concise, and you will never let any issues become stagnant or stuck again. Most of all, you will work with the choices of your employees and create a well-rounded, well-oiled workplace that runs efficiently and smoothly.

With Pre-Emptive Leadership implemented in your organization, you will no longer lie awake at night, worrying about the latest problem at work or how you're going to get it all done

In the Pre-Emptive Leadership System, every individual gets to decide whether they're going to be valuable contributors or not. There is no blame when things go wrong—only a sense of teamwork in getting things back on track. As a leader, you never say, "You didn't provide me with this" or, "You promised me that but didn't deliver." You make your expectations known ahead of time, so that your team members always know where they stand and what their choices are. They are always controlling their own actions.

The first thing you'll notice once you clarify expectations in the workplace is how much stress it relieves. Communicating specific choices with clear-cut steps brings a whole new attitude to the environment and makes working with people a joy. This feeling of freedom—from speculation, from wondering why team members are underperforming and so on—is energizing, and renews your sense of purpose. Instead of wasting the energy that was previously used on negative pursuits, you can focus on what you do for a living—which is also a major benefit for the organization.

What Right Looks Like: Clarifying Expectations

Common Questions—and Answers

At this point, you may have a lot of questions, as do many leaders trying to implement the Pre-Emptive System in their workplace. For example, you may be wondering:

- Does the Pre-Emptive Leadership System take a long time to work?

- How long will it take to get my "problem employees" back on track?

- Why don't we just tell our team members what to do from the start?

The first four steps of the Pre-Emptive Leadership System do not take long to accomplish and once you learn how to properly address front wheel, people-centered issues, you can smoothly and efficiently transition over to the back wheel when you need to. This should also take care of "problem employees," who are probably not the problem at all. Many of our client companies practice "Lean Manufacturing" or "Six Sigma," which are *back wheel* continuous improvement processes that align with Pre-Emptive Leadership. Pre-Emptive Leadership is a *front wheel* continuous improvement process for the people side of your business. Pre-Emptive Leadership is a very positive system, not an adversarial approach, and therefore just "telling people what to do" is not enough since it ultimately undermines motivation and the goals of a smoothly running workplace. In conjunction with "Lean Manufacturing" on the back wheel, you follow the process of our system on the front-wheel to ensure the inefficiencies or "muda" (waste) that are eroding the bottom-line are removed.

In A Nutshell

When productivity is low, instead of handing out discipline, you must first look for the root causes of the problem. Often, it's that employees do not understand what is expected of them; as their leader, it is up to you to clarify this.

Back wheel skills are just as important to Pre-Emptive Leadership as front wheel skills, but you must know when to appropriately employ each of them. There will come a time when you must step in and tell people what to do in order to get things done. This can be accomplished efficiently and productively by using our Pre-Emptive model.

As a Pre-Emptive Leader, you will bring benefits to your division, your organization and even yourself. By being upfront and clear about your expectations, you will sleep better at night and even perform the rest of your job duties better—which in turn will bring great rewards to the entire company as a whole.

What's Next?

"Accountability" means different things to different people, but for Pre-Emptive Leaders, it means making your own choices and taking responsibility for your actions, and expecting your team members to do the same. In the next chapter, we'll examine accountability problems in the workplace, and discover how the issue disappears once you implement the six steps of the Pre-Emptive Leadership System.

CHAPTER SIX
Instill Accountability

Reactive managers often cannot agree on what "accountability" means. Some believe it is a discipline; others simply say, "I'm holding you accountable" but do little to follow up and show that they comprehend the word's meaning. Without ensuring that what was promised was actually delivered, the reactive manager has a hard time holding others accountable and risks becoming the weak manager that allows employees to do what they please.

Whereas reactive managers are uncomfortable with accountability, Pre-Emptive Leaders understand its importance to a thriving, productive workplace. Leaders impress upon their employees that they can make their own choices and be responsible for their own actions—once the first five steps of the Pre-Emptive Leadership System have been put into place, accountability problems will practically cease to exist.

Confronting the Problems

As you move through the steps of Pre-Emptive Leadership, team members become accountable for their actions by learning how to make their own choices. Each step in the system provides employees with opportunities to improve or rectify their performance or resolve any problems that have arisen; by the time step six is reached, if these choices have not helped them to improve their productivity, this stands out to the leader as a problem to address.

Leaders are able to help most team members accept accountability for their own actions. However, in a reactive culture, managers are quick to discipline or even terminate these employees, rather than trying to find out what is causing their lack of engagement. We hear complaints about such situations frequently in our training: "We had this talented employee," a manager will tell us, "but we kept having to write him up for being late. Finally, we had to follow policy and let him go, and now he's working for the competition."

But Pre-Emptive Leaders know that there is another option. Instead of reverting right away to the back wheel, policy-oriented viewpoint, they allow these under-performing employees to resolve their own issues during the first five steps of the Pre-Emptive Leadership System. This helps the employees work on building up their own accountability and making themselves into more productive members of the team so that drastic measures such as job termination will most likely not be necessary.

Ninety-nine percent of your best employees could be viewed as "difficult" by another manager in another company. The best bring talent to the workplace, but they also bring ego, and they won't put up with reactive management. Instead, they'll go elsewhere to work for someone who "gets" and appreciates them—like a Pre-Emptive Leader in a competing company. They may make less money there, but they will be free to figure out for themselves how to keep their nonconformity from impacting others in the workplace.

Creating a Culture of Commitment

There will always be employees whom the Pre-Emptive Leadership System cannot reach—team members with goals that do not match

Instill Accountability

There will always be employees whom the Pre-Emptive Leadership System cannot reach—team members with goals that do not match those of the organization and who are unwilling or unable to change. It's important to point out here that these are not good employees with bad habits such as chronic lateness or inconsistent follow-through, or who have the potential to be top performers but have not made the right choices to get to that level—far from it. They are more like cancer in an organization, bent on draining all the productive energy from the workplace. We call these employees saboteurs. Unfortunately, these people are often at the heart of major problems in the workplace.

In a group of three hundred people, you will have five difficult people and as their leader, you might be able to influence three of them. The other two of the five will be the saboteurs. These people will choose termination rather than changing their ideas or behaviors to be more in line with the organization's values—unless they are "written up" by a reactive manager, which they take as a challenge. At that point, you may find them changing their tactics and continuing their destructive behaviors in different forms.

Saboteurs do whatever they can to negatively affect the efficiency of the workplace. They may break equipment, falsify reports or pit team members against each other with the intent to slow down production. They intimidate other employees and undermine managers. In fact, they can even *be* managers.

As an example, one of our client companies had a manager whose behavior did not fit the company's core values. A team member once went to the manager and expressed concern about her behavior. Needless to say, the employee's difficult conversation was met with hostility and threats.

"If you go over my head," the manager told him, "you can expect not to be here tomorrow." The manager was a saboteur going against everything the company stood for, and intimidated into silence any employee who tried to stop her.

Actions such as these are a form of unregulated negative response on the part of the saboteurs, who focus on retaliation by bringing chaos into the culture through dramatic events, reaction-getting tactics and blaming others for their own poor choices. They see their expressions of anger as a form of justice, and use them to control the environment in which they work.

When confronted with a saboteur's unruly behavior, others on the team tend to react to her instead of holding her accountable; that is, a saboteur's coworkers will respond to her negative comments with further negativity rather than telling her to stop, because they fear the chaos her retaliation may cause. This gives the saboteur exactly what she wants and leaves her team members intimidated and under her control.

When such dysfunctional activity becomes a daily occurrence, it's difficult for managers to tell who the saboteur is because everyone on the team can seem like one—angry, yelling and prone to using profanity in their frustration over what is going on. If the saboteur is uncovered in larger organizations, she might just be transferred to another division, where someone else will have to deal with her behavior.

Because reactive managers are unfamiliar with Pre-Emptive Leadership, they will not know that they should discuss the meaning of accountability with a saboteur, and that it might help put an end to this person's bad behavior. In the absence of accountability, the saboteur is able to cause a lot of damage.

So, what can you as a leader do to resolve such a toxic situation? Basically, just let the Pre-Emptive Leadership System work for itself. The system emphasizes team members controlling their own actions and interacting with each other appropriately and productively, and when all this is being done correctly, any saboteur in the workplace will stick out like a sore thumb. Whereas in a reactive environment, saboteurs can turn thriving teams into unproductive communities by making team members go dormant with fear or rabid with anger, in the Pre-Emptive culture there is no room for her destructive nature. She will naturally be "outed," and the problem will fix itself.

Instill Accountability 95

When we go into an organization where there's a lot of tension and low morale, we immediately implement the first two steps of Pre-Emptive Leadership in the workplace. When we do this, we notice immediate changes in the attitudes of all team members involved, especially those who we suspect might have been saboteurs in the past. Suddenly unable to push anyone else's buttons, they become aware that there is a level of accountability they must meet; at this moment of truth, they will either leave the organization on their own or do something so outrageously in violation of policy or procedure that there is no choice but to terminate them. Unable to cope with being accountable for their own actions, saboteurs will self-destruct.

Four Steps to Instilling Accountability

Reactive managers have trouble instilling accountability in their employees and, in fact, rarely even try to. Instead, whenever there is a policy or procedure violation, they go straight to verbal and written warnings; they threaten in order to make the problem go away without giving any real thought to why it happened in the first place.

Pre-Emptive Leaders, however, will first use the incremental steps of accountability to help instill ownership within their employees. Leaders know that verbal warnings don't necessarily instill accountability but instead give team members the feeling that management is working against them. Even when dealing with major issues, Pre-Emptive Leaders live by the core values of the organization and don't engage in judgmental or reactive behavior.

Here are four steps Leaders use to instill accountability in their employees:

Step 1: The team member needs to recognize that he's being counterproductive. When approaching an employee to discuss this step, a leader can say something like, "Up until now, we've really been working on getting you to solve your own situations, and we've both been very clear about what's been happening and any expectations we may have. Now, you have to recognize how your actions are affecting others."

How can you tell if an employee recognizes that he is part of his own problem? First, he has to be able to accept feedback from everyone who's been trying to work with him. Next, he has to acknowledge that he's made mistakes, and he has to openly listen to the perceptions of others. Third, he has to take that finger he's been pointing at everybody else and point it back toward himself. His communication must be truthful and authentic. Your intent must be to help, and to provide very clear expectations.

Step 2: The team member must accept responsibility. He has to stop pretending that there's nothing wrong and look at things he's done that have prevented him from getting good results. Instead of complaining about the lack of clarity, what questions could he have been asking? Instead of keeping his ideas to himself, to whom could he have spoken? Instead of trying to do everything himself, what other team member could he have included when planning for a project?

If this employee is able to tell both sides of the story, this is proof that he is accepting responsibility and that he is choosing to move forward on the steps toward corrective action. If he can't tell both sides, he is still finger pointing and blaming others and the next corrective action step to take depends on company policy.

Step 3: Now's the time to focus on solutions. As the leader, you are not interested in making this team member defend his past actions or try to explain his behavior. Instead, you want to move on and help him move on as well. For his part, he must stay focused on the expectations you have laid out for him and not take things personally or disengage from the conversation. The goal is to move forward in the right direction—and to do so together.

Step 4: Make a breakthrough. The individual needs to become a new and improved team member. Your goal is to leave him with the impression that you want him to be proactive and to succeed—but

Instill Accountability

that you also want him to be accountable, to drop the baggage and to get over past events.

At this point in the conversation, you must write down the commitments and actions you covered, review expectations and talk about future choices and responsibilities. This documented conversation gives your employee the best chance at either changing behavior or parting from the company on good terms. Hopefully, it will be the former; these steps work because you're not using them to create a wall, but rather to open lines of communication and help the team member get back onto a productive track.

Too often, instead of using these steps, reactive managers hold sit-downs with their "problem" employees and turn the whole thing into a management versus team member situation. Managers take things personally and become biased, and may even hold closed-door meetings with other managers about how they're going to get rid of this person. Employees who sense that they are working in such a hostile environment may lash out to prove that they can have the last word.

Pre-Emptive Leaders manage such situations entirely differently, with a people-centered approach geared more toward correction than termination. As a leader, you have the tools available to you to put progressive accountability in place without having to be the manager, the enforcer. Instead, by helping team members make their own choices and accept accountability for those choices, you are telling them that they own their problems, not you, and that they have the power to solve them.

In a Nutshell

By the time you reach step six in the Pre-Emptive Leadership System, if a problem employee's performance hasn't changed, you may have a saboteur on the team. Pre-Emptive Leaders don't jump straight to progressive discipline but instead follow the four steps of accountability and provide a chance for the saboteur to hold herself accountable, accept responsibility and make a renewed commitment to being a part of the team.

What's Next?

Stress in the workplace does not always come from being overworked. Often, it's caused by inefficient managers who spend most of their time managing instead of leading. If you aren't working with your people, you're missing a huge opportunity to outperform your competition. The next chapter will show you how leadership and people skills impact personal and organizational performance.

PART II

WHY YOU SHOULD CHANGE
THE WAY YOU LEAD

In the first section of this book, you were given the tools of the Pre-Emptive Leadership System. You understand the concepts. Now, perhaps you're deciding whether or not to implement them.

The decision you make will affect a great deal in your corporate culture. In this section, we'll share some case histories to help you understand how much is at stake. You will also learn how Pre-Emptive Leadership can have a major effect on your results and how it can make your life easier.

CHAPTER SEVEN
Outperforming the Competition

A key and immediate benefit—one that many managers do not realize—is that the Pre-Emptive Leadership tools will help you outperform the competition.

We've seen the system work in many different industries and many differently sized organizations with a variety of strategic visions, missions and objectives. There is one thing they all have in common: They need people to get results.

When you can control the way you interact with people, the size of your company doesn't matter. Nor does it matter if you work at a highly technical manufacturing organization or a professional services firm. All people in the workplace have common needs. They want to go to work, do their jobs and make a difference. They don't want to be involved with all of the "people problems" and drama that plague too many organizations.

Five Outcomes

A Pre-Emptive Leader will outperform the competition, with proper use of the system, in the following ways:

1. **Attracting and retaining quality people.** People are attracted to great leaders. They want to follow someone they believe in and someone who believes in them. The Pre-Emptive Leader provides such a positive and powerful influence, which allows people to flourish. As a result, the best in the business *want to* work for them.

2. **Getting more done with less people.** When you have a quality team, you'll find that it doesn't need to be massive—a few key, talented people is all it takes. Pre-Emptive Leaders build teams that can multitask, who can manage themselves and who take initiative to get jobs done, so the leader can concentrate on the big picture.

3. **Achieving performance expectations.** A Pre-Emptive Leader accomplishes his goals and exceeds what others expect of him. Because of his honesty and candor in his daily interactions with others, people know they can count on this leader, and reward him accordingly.

4. **Developing leadership teams.** A big part of being a good leader is trusting others enough to delegate priority projects. A Pre-Emptive Leader knows that he can't do it all himself. Instead, he sets up smaller teams within the department to spearhead different projects, areas or clients, and puts other Pre-Emptive Leaders-in-training in charge. Knowing that each team is in good hands, the Pre-Emptive Leader is thus free to focus on how the teams are working together, which ones are ready for new projects and so on—instead of getting caught up in each team's individual, day-to-day dealings.

5. **Establishing a connection with the customer.** Pre-Emptive Leaders understand that internal and external customers are the lifeblood of the company, and that unhappy customers are a big drain on profits. A Pre-Emptive Leader strives to keep all customers satisfied and succeeds because of the environment he has created for his workforce.

Letting the System Work

The Pre-Emptive Leadership System works in any industry and in any organization—it's effective in large corporations and small businesses alike. No matter the company's size, strategic vision, mission or objectives, Pre-Emptive Leadership will keep it running efficiently and productively.

We've seen evidence of this many times, in many different businesses. One that readily comes to mind is a national company that was floundering by the time we were called in to help. A victim of reactive management to the nth degree, the organization was disorganized, and its employees were disgruntled and dangerously unmotivated to do quality work that would benefit the business' bottom line.

Obviously, this company needed to implement the Pre-Emptive Leadership model across the board, at all its locations and in all departments. Using such a comprehensive approach, the company would be able to project a more cohesive, solid corporate image because everyone would be on the same page; everyone, from CEO to part-time employee, would know where they were going and how they were going to get there.

This sort of confidence undoubtedly helps a company earn the trust of its customers and even attract new ones in the process. After they converted to Pre-Emptive Leadership methods, the particular company we are talking about was even able to take customers away from its competitors—despite the fact that this company's prices were higher than other similar businesses in the industry. How's that for outperforming the competition?

With Pre-Emptive Leadership, this company's benefits just continued to grow and grow. Their safety records went from poor to stellar, and the quality of their products dramatically improved as well. Everything was going smoothly for the first time in a long time, and there was not one person in the organization that did not reap the benefits.

And then, unfortunately, everything changed. A new operations executive was brought in because he was the best at cutting costs and maximizing efficiencies. He took over all of the operations and, though it could have been an easy transition, his lack of leadership skills threw a wrench in the works. He'd come from a reactive culture and though he had a lot of management experience, he was not a Pre-Emptive Leader—he didn't know how to get the best from people.

The first, last and most fatal mistake that this new manager made was to not support the Pre-Emptive Leadership System in the company's culture. It wasn't a method that he was familiar with and, like many reactive managers, he was most comfortable doing what he thought had worked for him in the past. Therefore, he chose to put the Pre-Emptive toolkit on the shelf and in the end, it was the company that suffered.

These days, this national firm is nothing like it used to be. After two years, its turnover rate has gone sky high, especially when it comes to its supervisors. Its best people, fed up with the operations executive bringing back a culture of fear and a lack of trust, have all moved on, leaving the company in some less than capable hands. It's a sad story, but one that can happen in any business or industry.

From Manager to Leader

Most often things go in the opposite direction—from bad to good. This is always a thrill to witness, and satisfying to have a hand in.

Let's look at another of our clients: a company with a reactive manager who worked 80 hours a week but still always felt like he was behind in his duties. He rarely left his desk, not even for meetings, and a vacation was simply out of the question. If he even took a sick day, his facility would fall apart at the seams—he found *that* out the hard way.

Now, the problem wasn't that this manager's bosses placed unreasonable expectations upon him, or that his job was so overly demanding that he couldn't keep up with the workload. The predicament, we discovered, was that he was a micromanager: He had to keep his eyes on every single thing his employees did for fear that they would mess something up. He had little faith in them, and so didn't give them too many real responsibilities, such as ownership of their own projects or self-management of any sort. Developing leaders within his department and delegating tasks to them was never even a thought in his mind.

But let's not blame him entirely for this situation. After all, no one, in any company, works in a vacuum. Rather, he was a victim of his company's culture, which operated almost entirely on motivation through fear—of reprimands, of failure, of termination. There were little to no rewards for jobs well done, only relief that nothing had gone wrong.

This lack of training—the idea that had been instilled in this manager that he had to have a hand in everything his staff did, and that he couldn't trust them to make decisions for themselves—kept him working at least twice as hard as he really had to. He was endlessly putting out fires, as they say, which seemed to be constantly igniting around him; he worked long hours and most weekends. Because he was doing what the company had taught him to do, he felt like he was doing the right thing—as many managers in his situation assume.

Despite all his efforts, however, his facility was just getting by as far as the actual work went. His plant's performance rated average when it came to achieving its goals and was looked upon by upper management as being "okay" at best.

When we came into this company's picture, we knew right away that this manager was a prime candidate for Pre-Emptive Leadership. We knew that if he would learn this new way of leading his staff and dealing with the demands of his job, he could considerably improve his performance *and* the company's bottom line.

Initially, the manager was resistant to Pre-Emptive Leadership, but after he participated in a company-wide Pre-Emptive Leadership initiative, he was convinced to go ahead, take the risk and give it a try. He started by calling some small communication meetings and introducing everyone at his facility to the first two steps of the system. In no time, he saw the logic of the system and enthusiastically supported it because he knew it would benefit him, his team and the company as a whole.

By using the Pre-Emptive Leadership methods effectively, this manager enjoyed the five outcomes of the system that we discussed earlier. He attracted and retained good people; there was much less spoilage; there were fewer turnovers as well because team members no longer had to work long hours to keep up. Consequently, the quality of their work and their on-time delivery percentage increased, and in time they literally trumped their company's competition.

Eventually, this manager even got to help out other branches in the corporation, and garnered a promotion for himself. He did so well, in fact, that the company moved him to a larger facility in crisis, which he straightened out in no time by using the Pre-Emptive Leadership skills that we had taught him.

Learning to Compromise

Sometimes, applying the Pre-Emptive Leadership System is not about making radical changes, but coming up with a compromise that works for all parties involved.

This was the case in another company that we counseled—a high-profile, international professional services firm that we had worked with before. This time, we were called in to help resolve what they thought was an unsolvable "people problem," an issue of clashing personalities that was hindering their company's performance and throwing their competitive edge off track.

The biggest issue in this company at the time revolved around one of their star players, a managing partner whose personality and management style were really clashing with a top administrator. Their serious conflicts caused tension not just between the two of them, but throughout the organization; their disagreements put the majority of the company's employees off their game.

Now, the managing partner was threatening to leave the company altogether—and take his clients with him, which posed a serious financial problem to the business. The top administrator was nearing his breaking point as well, and if they both left, there would certainly be lawsuits and a lot of bad press for the firm.

And this was where we came in. After working for just one day with the firm's team members and the individuals involved in the crisis itself, we were able to determine that this wasn't an unsolvable problem at all, but an issue of faulty leadership and a lack of direction. They suffered from some serious reactive practices, but were all looking for a better way. When we told them about the Pre-Emptive Leadership System, they were willing and able to commit to trying it right then and there.

With the system in place, the firm that had become completely distracted by favoritism and turmoil turned itself completely around. Team members transitioned from fighting to communicating, from mistrusting others to taking responsibility for the team's success. As a result, all employees involved had more time to do their actual work.

On top of that, the managing partner and the top administrator worked their problems out, and both decided to stay with the company. This was great news: It meant that there would be no airing of dirty laundry in the media, and that a lot of potentially lost business was saved—all thanks to their commitment to utilizing Pre-Emptive Leadership, which showed them that it was more productive to compete with their competition than with each other.

Out With the Old, In With the New

The impact that can come from altering the way a manager leads cannot be understated. When a manager is causing chaos in the workplace, in all honesty, it's too expensive *not* to hold him accountable; the time that has to be spent on making up for his mistakes and running to keep up with production means dollars that are lost in the long run.

This was the case at a manufacturing facility of one of our clients. The plant's reactive manager was just not getting the results the company's executives desired, but he refused to use the Pre-Emptive Leadership System—he didn't see the need to change. His production was poor because he focused solely on back wheel topics and managed the facility through production numbers. He was so autocratic that he couldn't keep the good employees he had; those who did stick around didn't respect him enough to engage in his vision of how the workplace should run.

The result of this one man's mismanagement was staggering: The facility was in the red to the tune of $400,000 *every month*. Whenever these numbers came in, the manager pointed the finger of blame at everyone and everything but himself—the economy, the workforce, the cost of raw materials. It didn't seem to occur to him that maybe something *he* was doing was affecting the company's profits.

However, his boss—the regional manager—saw things a little differently. He was quite sure that the responsibility for the plant's growing deficit lay with the manager alone, and that something needed to be done about it. So, he talked to the firm's senior management team, which agreed that there needed to be a change in how this manager was working with his people.

When the reactive manager was told that things would no longer be done exactly the way he wanted, he decided that it would be best for him to leave the business. *No big loss*, thought the regional manager, and promptly replaced him with a manager from another plant who was already trained in Pre-Emptive Leadership.

This, it turned out, was the best move the regional manager and the management team could have made. The team was the same, and so were the facility and the equipment they worked on, but one thing was different: the leader. In three months the plant was breaking even financially, in six months it was at budget and by the end of the year, it was $1 million ahead.

All of this was possible because the Pre-Emptive Leader was able to go into this dysfunctional environment and create a culture of trust where there had only been fear before. He earned the loyalty of the employees by valuing their work and by being fair and responsive; in return, they gave him the best work they had ever done.

And that's the way to outperform your competition: with the commitment of your people, the one thing your competitors cannot duplicate. If you can win the hearts of your team members, they will come together to make sure that every project they work on is successful. That's how Pre-Emptive Leadership skills impact the bottom line.

Know Your Customers

There is another set of clients, consumers or patrons that you must also pay attention to: the commonly forgotten internal customers

Every company has customers. Maybe you call yours "clients" or "consumers" or "patrons." Maybe they're the people who buy things in your stores, or maybe they are other companies that contract you for specific services.

Whoever they are, and whatever name you give them, doesn't really matter. The only important thing is that they are the ones who pay you. They fund your business, your projects and your salary. You can probably see, in light of that, how important it is to keep these customers happy.

But, there is another set of clients, consumers or patrons that you must also pay attention to: the commonly forgotten internal customers. Simply put, they are the people who work for you. Your employees. Your team members or associates. The people who deal with those *other* customers and make sure that they are happy on a regular basis.

Putting it that way, can you see the importance of keeping your team members satisfied? Unfortunately, many managers do not—especially those of the reactive variety. They simply misunderstand that even if they don't have hands-on contact with their company's customers, they still have internal customers to satisfy. More so, they often do not understand the importance of valuing the internal and the external customers alike.

A client of ours had trouble seeing this distinction. The company's leaders used great Pre-Emptive skills with their external customers, but just didn't see the value of using those same skills within the company itself; in short, the employees were not valued as customers, too, and so their satisfaction was not deemed very important by those who ran the company. And as everyone knows by now, unhappy employees can lead to a lack of productivity and negatively impact the company's earnings.

As a result of this oversight, this client company's business is currently going through a downturn. The good people it once had have left their positions and, in many cases, have gone straight to the competition for employment. They've done this not out of a desire for revenge against the company that did not value them, but simply in search of an easier, pre-emptive way of working that could afford them the support they needed to be productive members of a high-performing organization.

The Big Picture

In the Pre-Emptive Leadership System, culture is everything. A leader must create an environment for her company, department or team that is encouraging, supportive and inclusive—not accusatory and reactive—in order to make her employees feel a sense of ownership about their work. There must be trust and commitment, even to the point of allowing any team member to question a decision or stop a product from being shipped if necessary.

The Pre-Emptive Leader sees the big picture, not just the small details, and so doesn't get dragged down by stress and micromanagement. By keeping an eye on the overall workflow and putting her team members' needs before her own, she is able to create a coherence that a reactive manager could never achieve. A reactive manager, in contrast, acts on her own self-interest and will last only a year or two in any one position before being cycled out of a progressive company. If she then brings her management methods to another company, the same thing will happen all over again; because she is not interested in building a culture of trust, her success, if you can call it that, will only come in short intervals.

The Pre-Emptive Leader, however, is different because she does not operate solely from her own ideas—she works with her employees to create a *team* vision that everyone can agree to. When there is a common goal like this, and guidelines that everyone can adhere to in a uniform manner, there will be no need to devote any of the staff's precious energy to figuring out who did what wrong or who is responsible for which tasks. Those things are already taken care of and are out

Outperforming the Competition 111

of the way, leaving time and resources available for better customer service and higher rates of productivity and profit.

To outperform the competition, a company must live its core values and embody the principles it claims to stand for. The problem is that many companies talk the talk—they have excellent mission statements, for example, or well-verbalized commitments to keeping their employees happy—but they rarely actually do what it takes to incorporate these words into their day-to-day business practices. They don't *really* trust their people; they say they do, but their behavior shows the opposite. This approach to leadership will get them nowhere because they are not really investing in and committing to their own core values, and making sure that their employees do, too.

People who think that the Pre-Emptive Leadership System is too coddling, and who do not believe that it produces powerful results, will not see what an enormous competitive advantage the system can create for a company or organization. They will be resistant to even trying it, much less making it a part of their professional lives, because they have grown comfortable and complacent in their old, reactive ways.

It's true that change is hard work—especially when we're talking about aligning your company's culture and the Pre-Emptive Leadership System. So, why *should* you change the way you lead? What's going to be in it for you, your team and your business?

Our answer to that is "everything." The Pre-Emptive Leadership System is proven to bring you the results you need to outperform your competition: less turnover; less waste, spoilage and shrinkage; fewer grievances; reductions in legal fees; and a *greater* ability to attract and retain top-quality people for your organization. The Pre-Emptive Leadership System just makes good, sound sense—and the sooner you start using it, the better.

In a Nutshell

Pre-Emptive Leadership isn't a touchy-feely, trendy type of management. It's a solid tool that will positively affect your company's results just as powerfully as reactive management will affect it negatively.

People want to be around positive leaders, and that is how the Pre-Emptive Leader attracts them. There is no time for negativity in this system; as a Pre-Emptive Leader, you know that concentrating on what's good will get you ahead a lot faster than seeing only the downside of things.

Pre-Emptive Leaders are fair, candid people—straight shooters, if you will. They are the kind of leaders that employees *want* to follow because they know they will never be steered the wrong way while under their direction.

What it comes down to is that people want to be led rather than managed. They want to be shown the way, not given a set of demands and left to fend for themselves. When they make mistakes, they want to be taught how not to make them again, not be threatened or yelled at. In short, they want a leader they can look up to—not a manager who looks down on them.

In this chapter, we shared several examples of clients who have used Pre-Emptive Leadership to outperform the competition, and those who wished they had. From each one, though, we can learn a lesson—namely, that it pays to be Pre-Emptive, and we mean that in a literal sense.

What's Next?

Often, implementing suggestions from the front lines drives profit-margin growth. Though it might be easier to make all the important decisions yourself, it's in your best interest—and that of your team and your company—to consult those who will be most affected by alterations to the workplace: the employees. You never know what sort of valuable input they'll come up with.

In the next chapter, we'll look at how to strike a perfect balance between trusting your own judgment and that of your team members when it comes to making and implementing decisions.

CHAPTER EIGHT

The Power of Pre-Emptive Decisions

In our line of work, we train managers across a spectrum of industries. Their jobs are different, their responsibilities diverse, but one thing is the same everywhere we go: Many of the decisions these managers make are out of balance.

Most managers fall into one of two camps when it comes to decision-making. First, there is the micromanager—an over-controller, someone who has to have a finger on every detail and a nose in everybody's business. A micromanager is wrapped up in his own self-interest and unable to give up even a small amount of responsibility to someone else; he makes all decisions on his own and rarely gets input from his team because he thinks that his opinion is the only one that will work. His employees do not trust him or any decision that he makes on their behalf.

In the other camp, there's the manager who suffers from "paralysis by analysis." She scrutinizes every detail she can get her hands on before being able to make a decision—which is usually a good thing

113

but, in her case, she gets so wrapped up in making the right decision that the process gets bogged down. Overwhelmed by the numbers, the reports and the opinions of others, her decision-making abilities shut down, and a solution never occurs.

Neither of these managers has any idea how much these all-or-nothing approaches cost them in terms of trust—not to mention money and time. Are you falling victim to this same trap? Are you, too, stuck in one of these camps, unwilling or unable to make decisions that will win over your team members and benefit your business?

The Trust Factor

The decisions you make and the way you communicate them in the workplace can greatly help you as a leader—or irreparably harm you. If you spend too much time soliciting opinions and trying to draw a consensus, your employees may grow frustrated with your indecision. Conversely, if you do not consult anyone when it comes to an important decision, you are sure to lose any trust that your team may have had in you to begin with.

A Pre-Emptive Leader is able to achieve a balance between these extremes—not too reliant on the opinions of others, but respectful of any advice that team members can give. Fifty percent of the time, he will ask for input; for the rest, he will get a sense of the situation, make the decision and then present it to the team members and rally their support.

Ask yourself where you fall in this equation. Are you a 50/50 decision-maker, like the one we just talked about? Or are you more like a 30/70, putting your own opinions above those of your employees? Do you think that a 0/100 ratio is more effective because you don't have to cloud the matter with other people's ideas? If so, we suggest that you go back to your Pre-Emptive Leadership principles and reconsider your stance because that sort of approach will lose you the trust of your team—an important factor in the decision-making process.

Because a Pre-Emptive Leader is able to earn high levels of trust, it's easy for him to meet that 50/50 balance with his team members. When he solicits their opinions, they know that what they say will be valued during the decision-making process; when he has to make a snap judgment on his own, they are confident that his choices will be sound, and that he will have all of their best interests in mind.

You can count this as one of Pre-Emptive Leadership's many benefits: When tough decisions come along, your track record will speak for itself, and your team members will trust you. This aspect of Pre-Emptive Leadership was verified by an employee at one of our client companies who confided in us about his team's manager, Dean.

The employee told us that he knew if Dean had to make a decision on the team's behalf, it would be a good one because he was constantly interacting with them and was well aware of their opinions and preferences. There was trust there, and so while the employees knew that Dean would ask for their input whenever possible, they also knew that when he didn't ask them, they would still support his decisions.

Pre-Emptive Leaders are able to handle decisions in such a way that their employees never feel devalued or left out, even when they are not directly involved in a decision's outcome. This is a testament to the solid relationship between leader and employee that the Pre-Emptive Leadership System builds.

Stepping Up

When it comes to making decisions, a Pre-Emptive Leader can be decisive without being autocratic. Although consensus is an option when it comes to decision-making, if that option is not available, Pre-Emptive Leaders can act with confidence and come to conclusions that they know will be beneficial to all concerned. They are not paralyzed without input from their team.

Times when the Pre-Emptive Leader may have to step up and make decisions on her own include the following scenarios:

When the decisions are made for the leader by upper management. When "corporate" hands down a mandate, it simply has to be done. Whether it agrees with your Pre-Emptive style or not, when the president of the company (who might be a reactive manager himself) says, "Jump," sometimes you just have to ask, "How high?" It's your job to carry out the decision and communicate it to your team, and you will do so with the integrity and honesty that your Pre-Emptive training instilled in you.

When it's a time-sensitive event or a sudden change of plans. A customer calls and needs a shipment by Monday. A client company pulls out of its contract, creating a need to rearrange your production schedule. Whatever the issue is, you have to face it yourself, right away, and do what's best for the company *and* for your employees. The most important part is that you communicate the change to your team members in as timely a manner as possible, and work *with* them to make the changes happen.

When there's a safety issue. If a faulty piece of equipment needs to be changed, or if a bin of material needs emptying, this isn't the time for collaboration. Instead, assign people to the tasks and thank them for helping to keep the workplace safe.

When there's a financial constraint. Layoffs, downsizing, the loss of a good customer—they happen to the best of companies. Unfortunately, in downtimes like those, you don't often have the power to make the decisions you want; you can't, for example, keep your entire team onboard and jeopardize the organization's future. Sacrifices sometimes have to be made, and sometimes you have to be the one to strike the blow. This is not a time to get opinions, but a time to act decisively and do what you have to do.

When a consensus cannot be reached. You've asked for input and you've gotten plenty of it, but what's good and what's simply a ruse to further someone else's agenda? Or, all twelve of your team members have different opinions—whose should you go with? In cases like these, you must be the tie-breaker, the one who puts a foot down and makes the final decision. It will be the only way that your team can move forward and we bet that, in the end, even

The Power of Pre-Emptive Decisions

117

those who would have preferred a different outcome will respect you for making the tough call.

Gathering Input

In many instances, by the time a leader comes to her team with a decision that has to be made, the employees have already come to their own conclusions and have simply been waiting for her to ask their opinions and give them the authority to act. This preparedness is an offshoot of the Pre-Emptive Leadership System; under the guidance of a trained leader, it's not surprising that the team will be prepared before they are even required to be.

In such a situation, the Pre-Emptive Leader will respond by listening to the workers' suggestions, giving feedback and rewarding honest communication. Then, she will take all the input and bring it to the drawing board, so to speak, where the final decision will be made. Knowing that the implementation of suggestions from the "front line" often benefits the company—through increased production, heightened employee satisfaction or growth of the profit margin—a Pre-Emptive Leader is wise enough to value these suggestions.

Times when you may seek to gather input from your team include:

When you need information from the experts on the subject. A person who is close to the decision—one who will be most affected by it—will often have the most important things to say about it. For example, if you're talking about changing a production process, why not ask the employee who works on it first-hand? Who better to tell you what the result of a change in the process might be? Remember, though, that other managers are not experts in the sense that we're talking about here. They may be great advisors when it comes to running a department, but when you need projections on the real-world outcomes of your decisions, go right to those that the decisions will affect the most.

When you want to ensure that team members feel included in the information loop. Sharing decisions with team members fills major needs on both sides of the equation: It gets you information that may be necessary to the decision-making process, and it keeps employees involved, invested and, most importantly, willing to trust you.

When you want some new ideas. Your team members are great resources—sometimes untapped, and just waiting for an outlet! Many times, even with the best Pre-Emptive Leaders, workers are too shy to come out and say their opinions, and are just waiting for you to show an interest in them. Draw these people out of their shells and you'll get a lot of ideas that you never would have thought of yourself.

When you have leeway on how the decision will be implemented. If you are considering a change that will not have to be rolled out immediately—such as work schedule alterations or bringing more people into the team—then you will have the time to discuss matters with your employees and should, by all means, do so. Gathering input this way can help you make the decision, as well as possibly influence how and when the decision is carried out, thus giving the employees a real sense of ownership in the process.

Talking to Your Team

The Pre-Emptive Leader knows how important communication is when it comes to her team, and so when a decision is made, she tells them as soon as possible. Even if she knows that the news will be unpopular, she will be upfront about it, stating that the decision has been made and addressing any questions or concerns that her employees may have.

Taking responsibility is key in such a situation, and the Pre-Emptive Leader knows that even if she did not make the decision herself—even if it was something handed down from corporate headquarters—she is still responsible for its implementation. This may be difficult when it's something that her team members weren't expecting or do not agree with.

The Power of Pre-Emptive Decisions

119

The challenge, then, is to get buy-in from her team members, to get them onboard with the decision. The Pre-Emptive Leader knows that she can do this simply by being honest, and by listening to what her team members have to say about the decision.

As an example, let's say that a company's owners have decided to change their employees' health insurance carrier. This could be a real hassle for many workers—it might mean having to change doctors, or an upset in their regular medication prescriptions.

Given this news, a reactive manager—himself displeased with the news of the impending change—might go to his employees and say, "It wasn't my decision, but someone from corporate said they're going to change our insurance to a new provider again." He might even just leave it like that, letting the team members fend for themselves as far as the logistics of the decision are concerned.

In contrast, a Pre-Emptive Leader will present the decision to her team members in as positive a light as possible. She will assure them that the corporation is not changing insurance carriers to make a profit for itself or to take benefits away from those who need them, but because the new insurance will provide better coverage for everyone. She will be honest about the downsides of the decision but will also highlight its good points because she understands how important it is to take responsibility for making the purpose of the decision clear.

It only takes a few minutes of your time to present information to your team members and allow them to react—following the NORM, STORM, FORM, PERFORM model we talked about in Chapter One—or even to meet with them in small groups, if necessary. It's your job to make sure that everyone leaves knowing *why* the change is happening and *how* it will affect the workplace and each of them as individuals.

Let the Values Decide

"It's not hard to make decisions when you know what your values are," noted Roy Disney, and he was right. When facing a difficult decision, a Pre-Emptive Leader will look to her company's core values for guidance, rather than following greed or her own personal agenda. She is aware that if she wants her choices to matter in the long run and be

> *When facing a difficult decision, a Pre-Emptive Leader will look to her company's core values for guidance, rather than following greed or her own personal agenda*

beneficial to as many people as possible, they must agree with the things that mean the most to the company—trust, integrity, quality, profits, and so on.

Working for your own interests when it comes to decision-making—instead of adhering to core values and letting your decision spring forth from there—may seem like a harmless way out when you're in a pinch. For instance, if there is a quality issue with your product but you're on deadline and within budget, what harm would it do to ship the product anyway, especially if no one would notice?

But the danger in such shortcuts is that once you start taking them—and getting away with them—it's awfully hard to stop. Soon, your sidestepping of the rules will turn into a habit that runs against everything the company stands for. And how good can you feel about your work when you know that you're undermining the values that you agreed to uphold when you took the job?

This does not occur to some managers, however. They simply focus too much on numbers, on the amount of product their teams turns out, to be concerned with the larger picture—the one that a Pre-Emptive Leader has in mind at all times. That includes core values, which hardly even come into play when all you're concerned with is cutting corners in order to meet production objectives.

We came across this problem in a company that we worked with not too long ago. This business had among its core values a desire to produce a quality product in a safe way, utilizing a culture of teamwork. These are great values and impressive things to strive for. For the most part, we found a great amount of respect for and support of these core values among the company's leaders.

However, there was one plant manager who just wasn't buying into it. He was overly concerned with the production objective but not so much with the safety and teamwork aspects and, not surprisingly, his behavior on the job was sometimes deemed questionable. In fact, it

The Power of Pre-Emptive Decisions

was discovered that he had been hiding rancid product, instead of admitting that he had made a mistake in his production and properly disposing of it. It was an unethical decision that made it clear he was not thinking about the long-term future of himself, his team or the company. It probably goes without saying that this unethical solution ended up costing the plant manager his job.

When team members see their managers behaving like this, it certainly doesn't inspire them to do any better themselves. They figure, if their manager isn't upholding the company's core values, then why should they? This creates a vicious cycle of *laissez-faire* attitude that can do real damage to the company.

With a Pre-Emptive Leader in charge, however, this will not be a problem. She will understand the ramifications of her decisions; not following the company's core values will not even be a consideration. A Pre-Emptive Leader understands that she does not work in a bubble, and that following standards is important to the decision-making process. It sets a good example for her employees and encourages them to get more involved in the process themselves.

In a Nutshell

When making decisions for the team, maintain a 50/50 balance: half the time, solicit input from your team and the other half rely on your own judgment. When you make decisions by yourself, your employees will trust you to do what's best for them because you've built a foundation of trust with them.

Communication is key when implementing workplace modifications, whether they are decisions you have made or mandates that have come down from the company's higher-ups. Let your team members know that either way, you are there to help them understand and implement the changes.

When making decisions, consult your company's core values and make sure that any choices you make are in alignment. Role model these values for your team members and you will gain their trust and respect even more, especially when it comes to the decisions you make for and with them.

What's Next?

The Pre-Emptive culture will attract the best employees to your organization and keep them there, giving your business a sustainable advantage that your competitors cannot match. The next chapter will show you how Pre-Emptive Leaders are able to align their leadership skills with the talents of their employees to build a top-notch team that is driven toward success.

CHAPTER NINE

How to Attract and
Keep the Best People

Other companies can mimic your production methods or copy your products, but there is one thing that you have that they will never be able to duplicate: your people.

When you go through the six steps of Pre-Emptive Leadership, you set yourself up to attract and keep the best people. These will be the employees who are as committed to the organization as you are, who understand the value of teamwork and who want to make their jobs—and the company—the best they can be.

Those who are not fully committed to being the best, on the other hand, will weed themselves out of the organization, simply because they won't be able to handle the new culture. This is okay; these aren't the players you want on your team anyway.

The Best People and the Bottom Line

For a long-term, sustainable advantage in the marketplace, your company has to have the best people—end of story. You can try all sorts of stopgap fixes to keep your business on the competitive edge but in the end, they will be short-lived if you don't have the right people implementing such measures in the first place.

When you have only the best people working for you—people whose values are in line with Pre-Emptive Leadership —you can expect improved outcomes and increased profits. The reason for this? Good employees take up less of your time and resources, leaving you in a better position to be a leader instead of a firefighter. When you don't have to run around fixing problems all the time, you can be more innovative, communicate better with team members and really work on building that foundation of trust.

In addition, when everyone is on the same Pre-Emptive page, the employees have more time and energy to devote to their work because they are not preoccupied by stress, complaints and trying to make up for others on the team who do not work as hard as they do. With these inefficient workers out of the picture, your team will produce more, and this will show in the company's final profits.

As we've mentioned before, a benefit of the Pre-Emptive Leadership System is being able to do more work with less people, which is a great way to save money for your company. You can then take those extra funds and channel them into sales, marketing, engineering, research and development, safety, manufacturing or any area that you choose. You could even cut the prices of your products, and pass the savings on to your customers!

Attracting and Keeping the Best

If you want change in the workplace, it all starts with you. To garner higher-quality employees, look at your own actions and ethics, and think about any improvements you could make to attract the type of team members that you want.

Some qualities of Pre-Emptive Leaders that many employees find compelling are:

- Personal values that align with the values of the organization. This shows a well-rounded approach to leadership and conveys

How to Attract and Keep the Best People

that you have a stake in your decisions—not that you just like to order people around.

- A true desire to see people succeed. Pre-Emptive Leaders want the best for their team members and will do what they can to help employees achieve their goals. This shows employees that the leaders are invested in their outcomes—that the leaders are part of the team, not just the people in charge of it.

- A positive view of the world. Pre-Emptive Leaders are confident in themselves, and they project that attitude to those around them. They see others as equals and treat everyone fairly, never speaking negatively about anyone or discouraging them from trying new things.

- An outward focus, but an inner drive. Pre-Emptive Leaders have innate wills to succeed, and they use that not for personal gain but to help their companies get ahead. They are not solely motivated by money or power, but by a sense of personal ambition that is expressed through betterment of their employees, their divisions and their businesses on the whole.

Ask yourself why people follow you. Is it because you're the boss? Or because you're so charming? We hope not; these are two reactive manager characteristics that sometimes manage to lure people in. But because these are such shallow attributes—not based on a foundation of trust and respect—the people attracted by them are often not of the best quality themselves.

Pre-Emptive Leaders, instead of relying solely on their personalities, create an air of authenticity around themselves. They project an image of confidence and success that becomes contagious; anyone who passes their way wants to get in on the good thing they appear to have. Pre-Emptive Leaders aren't interested in people following them because of who they are in the organization, but simply because of *who they are*, and that is why the best people are drawn to them.

One Is Good; More Is Better

If you can get good results just with your own Pre-Emptive Leadership skills, imagine what a bunch of you could do!

As a tool to attract the best people to your company or team, consider creating a synergy of Pre-Emptive Leaders. You can do this by basically duplicating yourself—by training more Pre-Emptive Leaders within the ranks. The more of you there are, the more the culture will permeate the organization, and this will create a strong signal that will attract the best potential employees as well as repel those who do not belong in the Pre-Emptive culture.

This sort of arrangement involves teamwork on a bit of a higher level—a concept that can be hard to grasp for some. Many managers, coming from reactive backgrounds, are more used to competing with their coworkers. They do not share ideas with or solicit opinions from anyone; they concentrate only on their own interests and are very competitive even with their own team members.

But when you work Pre-Emptively, this is not the case. You understand that part of your job is managing ideas, not just people, and that it will benefit the company to "share the wealth" and pass on the Pre-Emptive methods you have learned. Pre-Emptive Leadership thrives on mentoring and co-operation, and there is no excuse for not creating this culture within your department and *between* the organization's departments as well, and indeed throughout the organization.

This is what we teach when we introduce the Pre-Emptive System to our client companies: that it's not a flavor of the month management program but a comprehensive culture, one that includes everyone in the company. The best part about it is that spreading the message is not hard—just be yourself, a Pre-Emptive Leader, and through your influence and your actions, you will create other leaders practically without even trying.

All you have to do is hold your staff meetings, and communicate and interact with your team members. By modeling Pre-Emptive Leadership in this way, you're actually teaching your employees how to build trust, how to communicate better and how to resolve conflicts—in essence, turning them into Pre-Emptive Leaders themselves.

How to Attract and Keep the Best People 127

What this creates is a level playing field within in an organization, to the point that an outside observer would have trouble discerning who is in charge. The Pre-Emptive culture makes everyone equal: no managers, no workers, just a team of people working together toward a common goal.

Free to Be

One aspect of the Pre-Emptive Leadership System that really attracts quality people is how the process allows them to be who they want to be. When a company runs under the Pre-Emptive System, no one has to conform to a mold; everyone is free to have quirks, as many talented people do, and to express their own opinions and ideas.

This sort of acceptance of individuality is another aspect of the foundation of trust and respect that the system requires in order to work. When employees feel that they as people—not just as employees—are valued and even appreciated, they are more likely to feel invested in their work and in their company. Nobody likes to feel like a worker bee, like a nameless ID number who shows up, punches in and spends eight to ten hours a day doing work that goes unappreciated. Of course not—everyone needs validation to feel like their efforts are noticed and that they, as individuals, are valued.

By challenging employees based on their own strengths—say, for instance, periodically raising the bar for the highest producer on the team—a Pre-Emptive Leader can let that individual know that he matters, and that *his work* matters to the company. Methods like this go a long way toward building trust with team members because being challenged gives them a feeling of ownership in what they do. They can look at the end product and say, "I did that"—creating a feeling of pride that they have such a stake in the business.

Pay Attention to Retention

When you create a Pre-Emptive culture, you'll attract others who thrive in that situation as well. In fact, you may find yourself garnering new team members (and even leaders) from your competition who drove away their best staff with reactive practices and autocratic management. If you're creating a positive, Pre-Emptive culture, the word will spread, and you will begin to attract others who share your values.

We've seen this happen with our clients' companies. During one training session, we met an individual who had just been hired. He seemed innovative, and he demonstrated both high energy and flexibility—two fantastic factors for someone who wants to go into Pre-Emptive Leadership.

When we mentioned to this fellow that he seemed like a perfect fit for the culture we were creating at this organization, he said that several people had told him that already. The recruiter who had interviewed him for the job, in fact, had told him that this organization would provide him with everything he was looking for in a job. It seemed to us as though that recruiter had been right—he was a perfect match. You could call it a coincidence, but we believe that the right employee, job and leader had all found each other at last because of the power of Pre-Emptive Leadership.

When a match like that happens, it's hard to deny and you can bet that the employee in question will be so thankful, he'll do whatever it takes to keep his job secure. We've known employees in our client companies who received up to four offers a month from other companies trying to lure them away with promises of better compensation packages or more prestige—and they turned every one of them down because they were so happy with the company they worked for. They just could not imagine leaving such a supportive, positive work environment.

On occasion, it does happen that a team member will be swayed by other organizations' attention, and they will end up leaving for a position that offers more pay or a better title. We've seen it happen, but those who leave, in time, will come back to the Pre-Emptive culture that they loved in the first place. As they find out, money and prestige are no substitutes for trust and teamwork.

By the way, don't be concerned if headhunters are constantly calling your employees and telling them about "better" jobs. Consider it a testament to your Pre-Emptive Leadership—if you weren't so good, you wouldn't have such good people, and other companies would not be trying to win them over so stridently.

Looking Inward

A potential client company of ours was willing to use Pre-Emptive Leadership with its external customers, but not internally. Those running the company just did not trust their employees enough to treat them well; instead, they were constantly on the lookout for team members who appeared to be wasting company time, misusing company resources or taking advantage of the company in any number of other ways that they suspected, but could rarely prove.

The funny thing was that these managers knew what they were doing—they knew that they were treating their employees poorly—but they felt that they could not change their approach. The amount of change it would take to start leading Pre-Emptively was too far out of their comfort zone; they just couldn't fathom an overhaul on that grand a scale. As a result, they lost their good people to another company that attracted and welcomed all the talented individuals that this company was pushing away.

This client company was then left with a group of workers who were numb to their culture of distrust, and so were not very willing to do what it would take to make the company a great success. This caused an ongoing struggle to meet their production and profit projections. It also put a real strain on resources, as new strategies and flavor of the month programs were constantly being implemented in an attempt to keep the business alive and generate organic growth.

What this company failed to realize is how powerful just a little bit of understanding and teamwork can be. In a Pre-Emptive culture, everyone wants to work together—not just within departments but across the entire organization. There is no "stove piping," or silo effect like you see in many reactive companies; in the Pre-Emptive System, there are no walls between functional areas, and feedback across the lines is rewarded.

For example, let's say you are working in manufacturing and you notice that for whatever reason, you are not going to be able to fulfill a customer's order for a particular time period. You have one of two choices: Keep this news to yourself and just shrug your shoulders when the sales department is looking for the product to be shipped, or step up and tell the sales department that there will be a delay, so that they will not have to hear the bad news from the customer.

Which option do you think Pre-Emptive Leaders would choose? Of course, it would be the latter, not just because it's the right thing to do but because the leaders knows that their voices will be heard. In a reactive culture, in such a situation, the manufacturing manager may choose not to say anything because he knows that he will get nothing but grief from the sales department; they will only tell him that he *has* to meet the production deadline, no matter how impossible it may be, rather than working to figure out a solution together.

> *To attract the best people, a Pre-Emptive Leader must first examine himself and determine why people would want to follow him*

In a Pre-Emptive culture, on the other hand, there are no territories, no egos to get in the way. The leader of manufacturing looks out for his own numbers, of course, but he is also concerned with sales and customer satisfaction because he knows that they are linked together: When one is in trouble, it affects the other as well.

Because of this, the sales department's leader will not tell the manufacturing leader to simply go back to the plant and figure out what to do on his own. Instead, he will ask to hear more about the problem and offer to help however he can in order to resolve the situation. Rather than cut off communication in a time of crisis in order to save his own skin, the Pre-Emptive Leader will be receptive to and inclusive of anyone in the company who solicits his help because he knows that it's what's best for the organization as a whole.

In a Nutshell

Your people are your advantage over the competition. Treat them well and they will give you their best; when an employee feels valued, there is no telling how far she will go to make the organization a success.

The Pre-Emptive Leadership System will help you attract the best people as well as weed out those who do not belong in your company's culture. This frees up time and resources that can be better devoted to other, more lucrative areas, thus increasing the profitability of your business.

To attract the best people, a Pre-Emptive Leader must first examine himself and determine why people would want to follow him. Is he charismatic, able to get anything from anyone simply by using his charm? Or does he base his own success on the success of the team, creating loyalty by being involved, available and motivated?

Creating a synergy of Pre-Emptive Leaders perpetuates the system throughout an organization, making it stronger as a whole. When everyone in every division works together—instead of against each other—the entire company prospers.

The Pre-Emptive culture allows for individuality in the workplace, which creates a sense of investment in the mission for each employee. When she is free to express herself, a team member feels more comfortable in her job, and thus more willing to do whatever is needed to make the business a success.

Team members may come to you from other reactive companies that drove them away. Just remember that it's easy to fall on the other side of that equation as well—the more reactively you run your workplace, the more alienated your employees will feel, and they may start looking to other companies that offer more Pre-Emptive workplaces.

What's Next?

Why would anyone *choose* to be a reactive manager? Unfortunately, it's not always an option—a lot of the time, it just happens whether you want it to or not. In the next chapter, we will look at how people fall into the reactive management hole, and how, if that's where you're stuck, you can climb your way back out again.

CHAPTER TEN
Doing More of What You Love to Do

Why do you do your job? Something makes you get out of bed every morning and go to work, ready for another day of challenges and accomplishments. Is it the money? Bills that you need to pay? Prestige? Or have you followed a career path that truly interests you, and you actually like what you're getting paid to do?

Whether it's accounting, teaching, advertising or driving a bus, everyone has their own niche, their own area of interest that they desire to learn more about and excel in as a result.

When people grow and advance in their professions, they discover that "moving up the ladder" in an organization not only brings them more money, but increased influence over others as well. When they realize that they can now tell people what to do—and have everything done their own way—they sometimes become bosses, not leaders.

When this happens, they find that being in management is not all they'd hoped for. Instead of getting ahead, making more money and being afforded more respect, they are stuck in a cycle of firefighting

134 It All Starts With YOU

that keeps them from doing the work they love. This forces them into making poor choices and harboring resentments. In short, the focus has shifted from their *passion* to the *job*, and a reactive manager has been born.

Reactive Management Happens

Nobody wakes up one morning and decides to be a reactive manager. It's just something that happens, a phenomenon that sneaks up on you when you're busy trying to do your job and make things work the best you can.

When you're a hard worker, you often become the best at what you do. Then, all of a sudden, you are offered a promotion into management. A promotion is a sign that you're good at what you do, a reward for the hard work you've already put in; it's a natural progression in your career and you become excited about the possibilities. As a manager, you could have more influence, more input and more decision-making authority. In addition, a promotion could possibly bring you further career opportunities because you will be exposed to a whole new set of people and experiences. Besides, once you move up, you're bound to do it again. Sounds great, doesn't it?

These are all the ideals of a person with a naturally Pre-Emptive mindset—someone who wants to get ahead not just for his own personal gain, but because he believes that with more authority, he can do more good for the organization as a whole. Unfortunately, people like this are sometimes disappointed.

When Management Is Not What You'd Expected

If you're not already working in a company that has embraced the Pre-Emptive Leadership System, chances are that when you move into that managerial spot, you will not find the efficiency and opportunity you were hoping for. Instead, you may have problems you never even considered—dealing with your own supervisor's demands, shouldering the responsibility for other people's failures or shortcomings, and paperwork, paperwork, paperwork.

Doing More of What You Love to Do 135

And then, there's the whole team of people underneath you to consider—all of whom have different backgrounds, opinions and personalities. Some are in need of training that you may find you don't have the time to give. Others don't show up on time, or they bring their personal problems into the workplace, which can affect everyone's productivity; when one person lags, it drags the whole team down.

With issues such as these, your bigger-picture dream of benefiting the company with your leadership skills can fall by the wayside simply because you get caught up in the management of people. This can leave you feeling helpless and frustrated with your job; many managers have described this to us as not feeling "equipped," and that's an accurate word for it. Thrown into a management position with no training yourself, how can you be expected to show your team or division the correct way to go?

So while you might have once imagined yourself being a real team leader, the kind who interacts with employees and motivates them all to do their best work, you might now be finding yourself far removed from that idea. Instead of leading and teaching, you spend all your time reacting to the day's immediate problems and worrying only about what you need to get done. You don't have time to look ahead or think long-term when you're working overtime just to keep up with the daily demands. Instead, you're in constant reactive mode.

It's a Balancing Act

This is a tough situation to be in, for sure—when you love what you do but find yourself doing very little of it. Unfortunately, this is what often happens.

Take, for example, a group of sales managers who participated in one of our training sessions. Once, many of them were excellent sales-*people*, working with clients and enjoying what they did. Because of their achievements in those positions, they were promoted. Though they were excited to be able to get into management roles and teach others what they knew, they were inundated with team members'

136   It All Starts With YOU

motivational problems, meeting quotas, juggling administrative duties and going to endless meetings. They rarely had time for working hands-on with their staff, and their talents simply went to waste.

This is the challenge of balancing your management and leadership roles. Should you be the *manager*, focusing on the mechanics of the job, deadlines, personnel issues and timesheets, at the expense of your own skills? Or should you be the *leader*, working simultaneously to get ahead of this vicious cycle, build a foundation of trust with your team and pass on all of your valuable expertise in order to better the organization as a whole?

As you can imagine, Pre-Emptive Leadership provides time for both managing and leading. It allows you to be "in charge" while still creating an excellent workplace culture, one wherein everyone feels comfortable to be themselves and to get their jobs done right. When you can do that—instead of micromanaging and putting out those ever-present fires—you can focus on your own career's high payoff areas (more on those coming up). After all, you never know when another promotion could come your way, and you should be ready for it when the opportunity arises.

Breaking Free—It Is Possible!

If you're stuck in a reactive rut, it may seem like there's no way out, but we can tell you from experience that it's simply not true. No matter how overworked and overwhelmed you may feel, you *can* change the way things are going. It might not be simple, and it might not happen in a day, but it is possible.

Start by looking at the managers around you. Are they all in the same boat as you, or are there a few for whom things seem to go just a little bit easier? What about your friend who runs the operations division? You've both been managers for about five years, but he seems to be so much farther ahead of the curve than you are. He also:

- Goes home every day at a reasonable time
- Seems happy to come in again each morning
- Has a ton of energy
- Runs an upwardly mobile, self-sustained team

Doing More of What You Love to Do

- Makes managing people look easy
- Has plans for the future of his division
- Is known for developing leaders
- Handles problems within his department efficiently and confidentially
- Communicates clear expectations to his team members
- Does not avoid conflicts, but addresses them head on and works them out

What is this colleague doing that you're not? For starters, he is following the Pre-Emptive Leadership System.

But he didn't always. He started out in a reactive environment just like the one you're in—and he got out of it. He used to run around frantically, trying to get things done but feeling like he would never see the light at the end of the tunnel. And then he learned about the Pre-Emptive Leadership System, and everything changed.

Checks and Balances

Whether you're a new manager or a seasoned pro in the field, it doesn't matter—whatever stage of the reactive cycle you're in, there is still time for you to break free. If you're sick and tired of the way things are going, then make the decision that the way you've been running your company, division or team is no longer acceptable. This is a change that starts with you, right now.

To advance yourself into using the Pre-Emptive Leadership methods and skills, you must:

> **Take a look at the balance in your life.** Is your *work* life balanced with your *personal* life? Do you sacrifice evenings with your family, weekend plans with friends or hard-earned vacations for your job, putting in overtime hours that seem to accomplish nothing but bringing you more frustration?

Working within the Pre-Emptive Leadership System can help you find a way around this destructive cycle because, with it, you have a plan of attack that prepares you for situations that normally trip up a reactive manager. As a Pre-Emptive Leader, very few problems will arise. You will not have to stay late or come in early to try to get rid of the backlog that such issues used to create. This freed-up time prevents career burnout and brings balance into all aspects of your life.

Put people into your high-payoff areas. High-payoff areas are skills, actions or methods that will bring about valuable changes or results in the workplace. Team building is a high-payoff activity. Putting effort into cultivating a "one team-one culture" mindset now will benefit you and your employees. When you are faced with changes in production schedules, conflicts of interest or anything that breaks up the workflow, having unity among team members will make all the difference.

Establishing connections with your customers is also a high-payoff pursuit. So is providing training for those employees who require it, as well as being forthright in dealing with conflicts or misunderstandings. Anything you can do now to save yourself headaches and problems in the future can fall into this category, and every one of them is a valuable investment in your career.

Focus your efforts on leadership. Despite the positive aspects a promotion can offer, many talented people do not take on management positions because they see burnt out managers around them, and they don't want that sort of life. It's a shame, really—so many people with so much to offer, just wasting their skills because of their companies' refusal to step out of the reactive mold.

However, when Pre-Emptive Leadership trickles down from the top leaders to the supervisors and line managers, this scenario is completely different. Instead of potential leadership candidates looking at the culture around them and deciding that they do not want to be a part of it, there's a great sense of buy in; people want to be part of the Pre-Emptive culture because they see how positive and productive it can be.

The Pre-Emptive Leadership System changes the whole demeanor of the workplace. It even changes how people talk to one another. Instead of coworkers gossiping about each other around the water cooler, in a Pre-Emptive culture you find passionate discussions about how to best surpass the competition; the sharing of ideas between workgroups about how to best solve issues and get the work done; the buzz amongst plant managers about how many units they produced in a month. Healthy competition within the culture creates synergy between employees and leaders alike and having everyone on the same page like that does nothing but make the workforce stronger.

Unfortunately, you cannot transform from a reactive manager into a Pre-Emptive Leader overnight. It's a process, but one that is worth doing; just look at how well it paid off for your friend who runs operations, who goes home at a decent hour and has employees who respect him. The more you work on it, the bigger the payoffs become as well. Just continue to practice the six steps of Pre-Emptive Leadership and you'll start having more and more time to do the things that are really important to you.

Too Many Reactive Managers, Not Enough Leaders

Recently, while working with a large service organization, we found that the organization's team members had all initially gotten involved with the organization because of their passion for helping others. This was a great place to start, and one that we recommend everyone strives to achieve: When you love what you do, everything else can just seem to fall into place.

But even though these managers had joined up with this particular organization because of their love for the cause, morale within the culture was extremely low. How could this be? With very little investigation—most of the time, when a company is stuck in a reactive rut, the symptoms are easy to see—we found that the whole place was disorganized. There was no foundation of trust, just the underlying connective interest that, thankfully, everyone involved still held on to.

Unfortunately, however, we found that interest alone wasn't enough. To be successful in their pursuits—to effectively help people, as was the organization's mission—there had to be a sense of order, an atmosphere of encouragement and accomplishment that those doing most of the leg work could buy into, so that they could feel like their work was appreciated. There had to be not just management, not just people who assigned tasks, but *leadership*. There had to be people at the middle and top levels who took responsibility for projects and getting them done, who acted as role models as well as managers and supervisors and worked as part of the team to get the important work done.

But this was not what we found when we first entered this organization with the intent to show them the Pre-Emptive track. Instead, they had thirty teams with no leaders—just "top people" who tried to run things the best they could, but often found themselves simply butting heads with each other and not getting a whole lot done. Unskilled in how to get results through people, these reactive managers were making mistakes that they didn't even know existed, and were thus clogging up the system and actually working against the company's mission. In short, without real leaders in charge, none of the teams were getting anywhere.

The Answer Lies Within Us

Given the environment, it was no surprise that these reactive managers worked all day with their heads down, doing their own thing and feeling constantly afraid that there wasn't enough time in the day to get everything done. In the end, they figured that they alone would pay the consequences for the company's shortcomings because they failed to meet any number of requirements or expectations. As is characteristic of a reactive culture, they felt as though they had no support, and the stress this caused them did nothing but make their jobs that much harder to do.

Doing More of What You Love to Do

However, even under these less than ideal circumstances, the managers showed up every day because they still had that love for the work. They still wanted to help people and despite the roadblocks the organization sometimes threw up in front of them, they believed they were in the right place to achieve that personal goal. The irony of it, we recognized, was that all these people who were so committed to helping their customer were not doing the most fundamental thing they could do to achieve their goal: They were not helping each other. They were not working collectively, as a cohesive unit, in order to get the job done.

In short, this organization was a disaster of its own making, which was a shame because those who worked there meant so well. It had fallen into a trap that often plagues organizations where managers are too busy looking out for their "customers" to consider what is going on with their employees.

When we pointed this out to the board members, they were aghast. They could not believe that they ran a people-oriented organization and yet allowed their team members to be so unhappy, to suffer under the weight of workplace frustration and job dissatisfaction. Realizing their actions were opposing the core values of their organization, they were eager to learn a new way of doing things—one that would create a culture more akin to the work they did with their external customers that fostered understanding and teamwork and made everyone feel as though they had a stake in the outcome of their actions.

The Questions Everyone Asks

With our help, this organization went full steam ahead toward Pre-Emptive Leadership—though, at first, they did have their doubts. At the end of our training sessions the CEO asked us some challenging but very pertinent questions.

First, he wanted to know, "When we walk out of here, how do we know that things will really change?"

This is a common question. Our answer to it, no matter whom we're speaking to, is always the same: "The Pre-Emptive Leadership

System is no different than winning a tennis game, or writing a book, or pursuing any passion or hobby you may have—your results will depend upon your effort, and the more you give, the greater your reward will be."

The CEO nodded in agreement with our answer.

"That works for me," another employee offered. "But what if my leader doesn't keep up *his* commitment?"

Again, a common question. Those who are highly motivated to do their best and commit to the Pre-Emptive System want to know that the people around them will do the same—especially those who are in charge. Even the most self-motivated employees still need guidance, and in fact may expect a lot from their leaders. They just want to be assured that if they're going to give their all, their managers will be right there beside them, working just as hard as they are.

Before we even had a chance to explain this, however, one of the organization's senior executives jumped right in to answer the question. "We've been through a lot together," he said, "and that's not going to change. Those of us who are not up to the challenge will know it and will remove themselves from the situation. Everyone here cares enough about what we do to be honest about our own shortcomings, and how they affect our work. If someone no longer fits in with the operation, I trust that they will be forthright enough to say so, and to move on."

It sounded to us as though they were all on the same page, ready to jump right into the Pre-Emptive Leadership System and eager to get it started. Once they did, this team still got to do what they loved— and even got to do it more so with each other. Instead of just being concerned with their customers' needs, they became more sensitive to looking out for each other as well. They learned how to really build teams, how to create an atmosphere of trust, how to attract and retain the best.

With Pre-Emptive Leadership, they grew their organization to be twice as large as it was when they started, increased their service efforts and attracted more top-notch employees to help them achieve their objectives than ever before. Now, instead of standing around the water cooler gossiping about who is mismanaging what and which projects are getting pushed to the side, the employees buzz about the fantastic work they're doing with their clients, and how good it feels to make a difference.

In a Nutshell

Reactive managers are made, not born. Though you may never have pictured yourself ending up as one, it happens to the best of us. Don't fret—just remember that it's not a permanent state, only a rut that you can climb out of at any time.

It is possible to make the move from reactive manager to Pre-Emptive Leader. All it takes is a commitment to making it work—and a focus on your *passion*, not just on your *job*. Love what you do first and foremost, and you will find a way to be the leader that you need to be.

What's Next?

The culture of a Pre-Emptive company is one of its most important features—and assets. Keeping it running well and investing in it, even in the hard times, is what keeps your company ahead of the curve. In the next chapter, we'll find out what it takes to create a Pre-Emptive culture and how to keep it as the focus of the organization.

CHAPTER ELEVEN

Stay Ahead of the Curve

One of the most important priorities a Pre-Emptive Leader can focus on is the culture of the organization he works for. More than the tasks he has to get done every day, more than the personnel issues he has to worry about or the production quotas that he has to meet, the company's culture must be at the top of the list because when that isn't running well, neither is anything else.

More than just a management "style," the Pre-Emptive Leadership System is a comprehensive, workplace-wide method of facilitating trust and teamwork in order to get the job done—a pervasive culture made up of individual people working together toward a common cause. Pre-Emptive Leaders stay ahead of the curve by emphasizing this "people side" of the business, by investing in themselves and their people: the one aspect of their business that competitors cannot reproduce.

Investing in All the Wrong Places

When a company is operating in reactive mode, the people in charge often *think* that they are investing in the organization's culture because they have taken steps such as:

Training people. But they have only trained a few and, generally, only managers. When the higher-ups in a reactive company decide to put their money and time into preparing their employees for the jobs that need to be done, they often invest only in those who occupy supervisory roles. Even then the training provided is not sufficient and what they end up with is a group of managers who do not know how to *lead*.

Addressing problems as they arise. In a reactive environment, it's easy to ignore issues that may exist within the overall culture until a problematic situation comes up. In many cases, times of crisis are the *only* times when reactive companies will look at their own organizations' cultures. When they do, what they often find is an atmosphere of mistrust and dysfunction, an environment that is not conducive to teamwork.

Spending money. Reactive companies like to throw money in all sorts of different directions: capital expenditures, R&D, marketing initiatives, process improvement and so on. They figure that they must be doing okay if they have so much to spread around, but what they're missing is that financial gain does not always mean success for the company. They can put money into all the initiatives they want, but if they don't also invest in their people—with time and effort—then they are only half as successful as they could be.

In all of these measures, companies are cutting themselves short by not appreciating their one asset that truly sets them apart from everyone else: their people. By failing to train their employees and undervaluing their efforts, by ignoring problems within the culture and underinvesting in the areas that they should pay attention to most, these reactive situations are only made worse.

Companies generally spend a good deal of their resources investing in the technical parts of their business—in equipment or capital expenditures—when, to stay ahead of the curve, they should be investing in their people. Not if they have enough money left over after everything else is paid for; not as a second, third or even fourth thought, as though the employees are the lowest priority of all. Really, it's the opposite philosophy that brings success: Investing in people first brings about the greatest advantage that a company can create for itself.

Organizations that do not realize this are stuck in a reactive mode and need to realize that their people—and thus their culture—can be their tool for achieving maximum performance, if only they give them the attention and the backing that they need.

Going After the Great Return

There are many reasons why companies might not focus on their greatest assets—namely, their people and their culture. Perhaps they are short-staffed, and just don't have the time; perhaps they are going through a bit of a bust period, and don't have the capital to distribute as freely as they once did. Many companies might even tell you that they'd never considered putting more thought into what their employees want—there have been few employee complaints, so they've figured that everything must be going okay.

What they don't seem to realize is that maybe things are *not* okay. Maybe employees are not complaining because they feel that their grievances will fall on deaf ears, or because there is just too much to complain about—they feel like they're on the losing end of the fight before it even begins. Situations like this—when team members don't feel as though they can speak their minds, especially when there are problems—make it easier for those in charge to simply look the other way and pretend that everything is going well.

Of course, this is something that should never be done. A problem ignored is a problem that will fester and grow over time; disregard issues that are going on today and by next week, they could be ten times harder to resolve.

This is not a problem for a company operating under the Pre-Emptive System, however. Pre-Emptive companies take the time to listen to what their people have to say and even act on their employees' recommendations for solving problems. With this simple act, companies can create a great sense of investment in the people who work for them, which encourages the employees to do their best when it comes down to producing results. We've said it before, and we'll say it again: When employees are happy, their willingness to give their all for the sake of the company's mission will be limitless.

Pre-Emptive companies realize this. They know that if everyone is on the same page, working toward the same goals with the same enthusiasm, there is potential for great return. They know that there must not be any sort of performance gap—no conflicts between the behavior of the people in the organization and the company's stated goals—in order for the company to accomplish what it needs to.

If such a situation exists—if a performance gap rears its head in the workplace—it takes a lot longer to get things done because this gap creates holes in the structure that allow for enormous waste of the company's resources. Pre-Emptive Leaders aim to never let this happen by committing great focus on teamwork, building trust and encouraging achievement. In short, they keep their eyes on the company's culture and in doing so, set themselves up for the greatest return possible.

A Culture of Success

Once Pre-Emptive methods have been put into place, companies find that they are able to achieve sustained success. They do this by honing in on Pre-Emptive culture in the following ways:

Making culture part of their performance objectives. Company-wide and on an individual basis, the people within Pre-Emptive cultures are held accountable for adhering to and upholding the company's core values. Among these should be trust, unity, and commitment to excellence—all factors of the Pre-Emptive

Leadership System. Including these values in the company's stated mission brings extra focus, and sends a message to all involved of their importance.

Ensuring that investment in the culture is a priority. It's easy for a company to show its employees how much it values them when times are good. When money is flowing, companies are able to give out bonuses or start initiatives to improve the workplace. However, when things are not going so well—when the market is down and products are not selling like they used to—it's also easy for those in charge to pull in the reins, to close up the company's wallet and leave the employees wondering what they did wrong to bring all the good times to an end.

It's important in situations such as this—when an organization may be going through a "down" time—that the Pre-Emptive culture continues as it always has. This willingness to allocate resources solely to sustain the culture is what separates the truly great companies from the rest. Pre-Emptive companies understand that strong cultures are the quickest way to move ahead, restructure and implement a new business strategy.

Training Pre-Emptive Leaders. There is no better way to perpetuate the culture than to train more of the organization's people to be Pre-Emptive Leaders. The more leaders there are company-wide, the more pervasive the culture will be; as discussed earlier, a network of Pre-Emptive Leaders across divisions creates a powerful synergy that allows for a free exchange of ideas, as well as mutual support and respect. By allocating resources to helping its best and brightest become versed in the Pre-Emptive steps, the company is making an investment not just in its people but in itself.

A Pre-Emptive culture receives support from the very top of the company via not only words but actions—the examples above are just a few of the ways in which the leaders of a Pre-Emptive organization can

150 **It All Starts With YOU**

foster the system's culture throughout the entire workplace, from the higher-up divisions down to each individual employee.

An example of this level of support was shown in one of our client's training sessions when one of the participants received an urgent call from his manager, who told him to fly back to corporate headquarters right away. There had to be an emergency meeting about an issue that had arisen at one of the company's plants and was severely affecting their product's quality.

Now, the participant who received this call was a pretty important member of the company—he was the "go-to" guy in times of crisis, and his manager hadn't thought twice about calling him out of our training so that he could fix whatever problem their reactive culture had created.

This participant, however, *did* think twice about it. From the beginning of the training session, it had been apparent to us that he was interested in Pre-Emptive Leadership and already seemed to have a grasp of its most important concepts and how it would impact his organization.

"I think it's important for me to stay here and finish the training," he boldly told his boss. "There are other people there who can handle the problem. And I assure you that I'll follow up with all of them as soon as I'm done here."

His manager might have been a little put off by this suggestion, but we were certainly proud of this leader's commitment to his development. He instinctually saw the big picture and acted on it instead of reacting to a crisis and running off frantically to be the expert that could save the day.

In the end, his manager consulted with the CEO and called back with the decision: "The CEO said he wants you to stay in training," he reported. "There's nothing more important that you could be doing right now than learning about how to implement the Leadership System into your division. We'll find someone else to address the quality issue back at headquarters."

When the participant went back to his company, he did follow up on every issue that had arisen while he was away—and started to put into place new systems to ensure that the same problems would not come back into play. Knowing that he had the full support of the CEO, he felt confident as he went ahead and began to integrate the Pre-Emptive tools and methods into the organization.

The Three Levels of Culture

In all the work we've done, in all the companies we've advised and counseled over the years, we've gotten a good look at what really goes on in workplaces. We've seen the ways in which things run, the methods people use to communicate with each other and the many factors that can cause a culture to either break down and stop functioning—or grow, flourish and thrive.

We've found that there are three distinct levels of culture in any given workplace:

1. **Scrambling**. In this culture, everything is always a day late and a dollar short. No one—employees, leaders, CEOs—feels like they can ever get ahead. Meeting simple day-to-day priorities is a struggle. There is no looking toward the future because all the energy is spent on taking care of today—and, often, yesterday as well.

    A Scrambling culture consumes a lot of energy from the company and its employees, who are constantly engaged in fighting fires and scurrying to get things done. This energy could be better spent on improving working conditions, on striving toward company core values, on meeting and exceeding expectations. Instead, it is squandered on problems and misunderstandings that do nothing but hold the company back.

    Any attempts to break out of this Scrambling cycle are akin to firing a bullet from a gun: They soar high and give off a lot of noise but in the end, they fall to the ground and stay there, quickly spent and no longer of any value. Rather than coming up with solutions that can effect real change and improve the way things are done, the managers in this culture only have time for fast fixes, which, in the end, create more of the same—more scrambling.

2. **The Old School**. This culture is based on good, old-fashioned fear of that one person who has the power to make you or break you work-wise: *the boss*. The reason why he is feared? Because he believes that people need to be managed—not like employees, but like children who need to be watched every minute and scolded when they're bad. He has little trust in anyone and has no problem showing it. He doesn't really care what you think if you work for him; his opinion counts the most since he is the one "in charge."

    Despite this, an Old School culture is not entirely unsuccessful. It does have its hard-won achievements, but often finds itself taking two steps back for every one pace it moves forward. Perhaps this is because there is little passion for the work, and little loyalty to it as well. The turnover rate in an Old School culture is generally high—as is the cost of grievances and related litigations, both of which draw resources away from the areas that really need them.

3. **Ahead of the Curve**. The leaders in this culture believe that people come first, and that is what keeps them ahead, plain and simple. They also believe in high standards and refuse to bow to the mediocrity that other cultures offer; they know that "there's never enough time" and "that's not in the budget" are just excuses that other managers use to hold themselves back.

    In a culture that is Ahead of the Curve, every team member's expertise is valued and encouraged. Everyone's ideas are heard and considered, no matter their status or standing in the company. Leaders approach their employees with genuine concern and care, and that attitude permeates everything they do, as well as the culture itself. There is nothing fake here, and it shows in the great returns and impressive success that those in such a culture enjoy.

As we said before, companies generally fall into one of these three categories but sometimes it is possible to fluctuate between the first two. Scrambling and Old School cultures do have some overlapping features and companies can find themselves meandering between the two in any number of reactive ways.

The culture that is Ahead of the Curve, however, is in a class all by itself. There are no similarities here with the other two cultures. Those companies that are within this realm have made the leap and pulled out so far ahead that the other two cultures cannot even hope to catch them.

Management Versus Leadership Style

Whereas each workplace can fit into one of the three cultures we describe above, so can each workplace's managers or leaders. We have found in companies we have worked with that those who are in charge can usually be put into similar groupings.

The **Scrambling** manager lives paycheck to paycheck and often feels as though he's on the edge of disaster. He focuses on activities—getting the boxes on the trucks, processing new orders—rather than on results such as achieving goals on time and on budget or planning the next strategy for increasing on-time delivery. In other words, he lacks the "big picture" viewpoint.

Eventually, the Scrambling manager will fall so far behind in his duties that he will be demoted. In frustration, he will leave the company and find a job someplace else, where he can start his scrambling process all over again.

The **Old School** manager pays her bills and has some savings to fall back on, and so doesn't stress out about money. She focuses on numbers, facts and data and almost completely ignores those who work for her. The figures are more important, after all, because she thinks that they show her what's *really* going on in her department.

154 **It All Starts With YOU**

Although an Old School manager can produce constant (yet not *significant*) results, there is no real strategic plan when she's in charge. She tends to follow flavor of the month trends as far as supervisory methods go; whatever new thing she hears about from other reactive managers or from the how-to books she's fond of reading is what she goes with. When it doesn't work, she simply drops it and moves on to something else.

Ahead of the Curve managers—the Pre-Emptive Leaders—are often viewed as "lucky" by their colleagues because they seem to have everything in order, and their achievements are often impressive. But this is no result of luck; far from it, these leaders have worked hard for their success, leveraging their greatest assets—their people—to achieve the greatest returns.

The leader who stays Ahead of the Curve does not toy with management styles that he reads about in books or magazines. He sticks to what he knows will work because it has been tested and proven: balancing his company's or division's front and back wheel priorities, building trust and supporting his team members in everything they do.

When utilizing the "one team, one culture" approach to leading, a Pre-Emptive Leader has many options. In life and in work, many doors are open to him; it's only a matter of choosing what he wants to do, or where he wants to go next.

Building a Culture

To create a successful Pre-Emptive culture, leaders must first have a personal leadership plan. They must understand their own strengths and weaknesses, and know where they're going as well as how to get there. They must understand that their interactions with their people will be of foremost importance and based on that should ask themselves questions such as:

- How am I interacting with others in relation to the core values of the company?
- How am I perceived in staff meetings?
- When I leave voicemails, do they communicate what I want them to? How about my e-mails?

In addition, Pre-Emptive Leaders must be willing to make changes

Stay Ahead of the Curve

within themselves to help the overall culture. They must be able to scrutinize themselves objectively and admit when what they're doing is just not working.

Some questions that can help in this area are:

- How can my actions be more aligned with our company's core values?
- In what areas do I need to develop my skills so that I can be a more effective leader?
- What are my talents? What areas of leadership do I need to leverage?
- How can I more positively influence the people around me?
- Overall, do my words match my actions?

A large part of being a Pre-Emptive Leader is looking toward the future. A leader is always a few steps in front of what's going on right now, planning for what comes next and trying to pre-empt any problems that can pop up on the horizon. To continue with this foresight, there is but one question that Pre-Emptive Leaders can ask themselves, and it's something that they should think about every day:

- What's the most valuable thing I can do right now to stay ahead of the curve?

Helping the Culture Grow...and Grow...

At the same time that Pre-Emptive Leaders are making their self-evaluations and improving themselves personally in order to build a better culture, they also have to work on a plan for team development. A Pre-Emptive environment, after all, will not thrive without a good, solid team to keep it going.

To form a plan that will ensure a Pre-Emptive culture through strong team building, a leader can utilize the following methods:

Building trust by holding periodic discussions about the company's core values. Leaders can talk with their team members candidly about how their actions align with the organization's core values, how successful they are as a team at meeting them—and how they can do so more efficiently.

Increasing communication by talking to each other in a common language. There should be no "manager speak" here; during discussions, everyone should feel as though they are conversing with their equals in plain language that everyone can understand. Leaders should hold monthly meetings to allow team members to discuss their problems and successes in the area of interpersonal communications—not just to discuss task-related priorities.

Resolving conflicts openly and presently. This can be accomplished by addressing problems or misunderstandings as soon as they arise, and by dealing with them fairly and confidentially. At a minimum, leaders need to schedule a monthly team meeting to openly discuss any lingering tensions or misunderstanding that exist and generate team and individual action plans in order to resolve them.

Encouraging team members to motivate each other. Leaders make it clear that everyone is responsible for motivation. They encourage their employees to communicate their needs to one another and work on incentives together. This is team building at its best, and it can be a powerful tool if implemented correctly.

Helping team members clarify their expectations of one another. In the Pre-Emptive culture, there are no hidden agendas. No one goes home at the end of the day unsure of what everyone else thinks of them, or scared that they're not doing what they're supposed to. Instead, constant communication about expectations, goals and rewards lets everyone know where they stand and what to expect.

Allowing team members to hold each other accountable. Everyone on the team should know that "checking up" is not just the manager's job; it's the responsibility of everyone involved, from the leader on down. Anything less works against productivity by creating resentment and frustration. A team is only as strong as its weakest member, and it is the job of the *entire* team to influence that weakest member to succeed.

Pre-Emptive teamwork is a result of Pre-Emptive Leadership. The two concepts are intertwined, and the former depends upon the strength of the latter to succeed. Though there is a level of ownership accounted to each member of the team within the Pre-Emptive culture, the process begins with the leader, and is sustained by his words and actions. Knowing that everything he says or does will have an impact on the team's morale and productivity, he must have an ethical code of conduct—for himself and for the team—in order to maintain the advantage that the Pre-Emptive Leadership culture creates.

In a Nutshell

Focusing on culture is one of the most important tasks that Pre-Emptive Leaders can undertake. Emphasizing this "people side" of the business and investing in themselves and their people keeps them ahead of the curve when it comes to outperforming the competition.

Concentrating on culture takes more than just training the company's managers and putting money into projects and initiatives. Though many businesses feel that they are doing well by doing these things, they are fooling themselves—and their employees know the difference.

Success is created by honing in on the company's culture through performance objectives, investments and training. Pre-Emptive companies that focus their efforts from the top down on these people-centric concerns enjoy the most success and the greatest returns for their business.

There are three general categories of management that companies fall under: Scrambling, Old School or Ahead of the Curve. Pre-Emptive Leaders set themselves apart in the last category by focusing on their people and their culture.

Pre-Emptive Leaders are introspective and self-critical in order to keep themselves on top of the game. By changing their own actions as needed to be more effective in their positions, and by constructing and following through on plans to build and sustain their organizations' culture, they set the foundation for their business' future success.

What's Next?

Is it possible to have *fun* at work? As a Pre-Emptive Leader, it's imperative—along with making money and getting a good night's sleep. In the next chapter, we'll look at what it takes to fulfill all three of these needs on an ongoing basis.

CHAPTER TWELVE

Have Fun, Make Money and Sleep Well

In over twenty years of researching, working with and training others in the Pre-Emptive Leadership System, we've had the chance to observe many dynamic leaders and find out what made them tick. Many thrived on challenges and did best when the work was more difficult; others lived for the teamwork aspect of the Leadership System and truly shined when pulling their team together for informal but informative meetings.

No matter the leader's forte, however, three traits—we could call them "objectives"—have long stood out to us as common to most Pre-Emptive Leaders. These are the things that keep them going, keep them excited about their jobs and on top of their game—for without fun, money and the peace of mind that lets them sleep well at night, what kind of leaders would they be?

Fun Is Serious Business

For Pre-Emptive Leaders, having fun comes naturally—and we're not talking about telling jokes or riding roller coasters. Instead, our sense of "fun" means the way in which leaders approach their jobs and their lives—with ease, looking forward to the next challenge and excited about what they're doing. By utilizing this mindset, Pre-Emptive Leaders are able to make a game of even the most difficult situations—and envision themselves up at bat, at the bottom of the ninth, with bases loaded, and fully prepared to hit a grand slam.

They can take vacations with confidence, and not have to worry that they will return to a business in ruins

This sense of readiness makes life—thus work, and vice versa—easier for Pre-Emptive Leaders. When they are relaxed, ready and confident that they will come out on top, their people see it and are able to feel greater trust in what their leaders are doing. Because of this chain reaction, there are dramatically less "people problems" in the Pre-Emptive Leadership culture—employees have faith in their leaders and are more willing to work *with* them, not against them.

With less "people problems" to worry about, Pre-Emptive Leaders have the time to do what they love—be it hands-on training with their team members, implementing initiatives to improve the workplace or simply perfecting their own golf game. After all, with fewer problems to fix at work, Pre-Emptive Leaders have no need to stay late at the office, and are more free to pursue their own personal interests.

Some Pre-Emptive Leaders find that they enjoy using their freed-up time to contribute to their communities, which increases their opportunities for influencing others. Many are also thrilled to learn that with things running so smoothly at work, they can take vacations with confidence, and not have to worry that they will return to a business in ruins.

In this sort of organized but easygoing culture, leaders can enjoy the full benefits of the Pre-Emptive cycle. They can have real rapport with their people, who are themselves inspired to be motivated, to hold themselves accountable for their actions and to work without unproductive conflict. The leaders and the employees are a tight team, intuitive about each other's needs—and that's a practice that the team members learned from the top, right from their leader himself.

Pre-Emptive Leaders are known throughout their organizations for their genuine smiles and easy laughs, as well as for their approachability—even people from other divisions know that they can talk to a Pre-Emptive Leader about anything. And this friendly demeanor isn't just an act; Pre-Emptive Leaders really do seem happier because they are able to make the most out of life instead of getting caught up in the unnecessary negativity and pressures that we all encounter every day.

The Reward: Money

Pre-Emptive Leaders are not focused on money—but money *is* the outcome of their tremendous success.

Great things happen to Pre-Emptive Leaders because they attract positive outcomes for themselves. Rewards, promotions, raises—whatever they desire, they can have because they're following an effective, proven system. They work hard, they do things right and they reap the benefits. They are successful, though many reactive managers might look at them and sourly call it "luck."

For all the work that they do, Pre-Emptive Leaders are compensated well. They generally fall within the high end of the pay scale in their field—their employers recognize their value and want to keep them on the team, and so they make sure that they are rewarded—financially—accordingly.

But as we said before, money is not the primary focus for Pre-Emptive Leaders. While they do generally enjoy the nice lifestyle a good salary can provide, their focus is usually more far-reaching. Instead of thinking about the new gadgets they can buy or where they can invest their money next, they concentrate on what they can do to make a situation better for all involved, or how they can provide more value themselves. They are not managers who talk only about themselves and how much money they make, but leaders who are secure in what they have and so instead use their time looking out for others.

This is only one of many reasons why people are attracted to Pre-Emptive Leaders—and only one reason why these leaders are so highly marketable. Demand for excellent leadership is high in all areas of business, and so it's no surprise that Pre-Emptive Leaders often receive calls from competing companies who want what they have to offer. It's also no surprise that, as valuable as Pre-Emptive Leaders are, they are often already meeting their financial goals within their current organizations.

Nothing Beats a Good Night's Sleep

Perhaps one of the best parts of being a Pre-Emptive Leader is knowing that the work you choose to do each day is in alignment with your personal convictions and values. Such internal synergy can create a sense of great calm—what we like to refer to as the ability to sleep well at night, knowing that everything is as it should be.

Pre-Emptive Leaders possess specific mindsets that allow them to rest at ease in this way. Among these winning attitudes is the ability to:

Refuse to live a divided life. Pre-Emptive Leaders practice what they preach and follow a holistic approach, taking into account what their organization stands for *and* what they think is the right thing to do. Many reactive managers cannot believe that such an agreement is possible, and so spend their days wrestling with demands that go against their own personal standards—such as being asked to ship low-quality products or knowing about the unethical behavior of other managers but being powerless to do anything about it. Such inner struggles lead to sleepless nights, and this is why Pre-Emptive Leaders refuse to work in such an unnecessarily frustrating environment.

Choose to do the right thing. Pre-Emptive Leaders live their own personal missions, and so when confronted with pressures to make choices that they do not fully stand behind, they do not give in. Even if it means leaving their present organization and finding a company whose ethics are more attune to his own, a Pre-Emptive Leader is not afraid to stand up for what he believes is right, and has the courage to act on his convictions.

Have Fun, Make Money and Sleep Well

Practice ethical behavior at all times. Even when no one is looking, Pre-Emptive Leaders are doing the right things. Unconcerned with what others think of their choices, they opt for the high road, rather than the path of least resistance; it's a part of who they are. Examples of such ethical leaders—and companies—exist throughout history, but one that immediately comes to mind is Johnson's Tylenol. When the company's product had to be recalled, the leaders made the tough—but *right*—decision to be honest with the public about what they were doing and why, rather than trying to cover it up. Though they could have taken steps to protect their brand at all costs, they chose instead to put public safety first and as a reward for their honesty, their brand has since become even more trusted by consumers. This just goes to show that while doing the right thing might be difficult and even expensive in the beginning, in the long run, the paybacks can be significant.

Pre-Emptive Leaders gain their own individual "paybacks" for their integrity and for their ethical choices in the workplace. Not the least of these is the absence of enemies, or those who would conspire to keep the leader down and make the culture of the workplace hostile and uninviting. On the contrary, because team members know that their leader will make the choices that are right for all of them, they offer her their full backing and support, and everything is done with an air of good will.

Pre-Emptive Leaders know how invaluable this help from employees can be, particularly when making tough decisions. In fact, it is just another part of the mindset that helps them rest easy at night, because they know that whatever will arise tomorrow, they will be able to face it head on—and solve it in the quickest and most beneficial way possible.

In a Nutshell

Pre-Emptive Leaders bring a sense of ease—indeed, a sense of fun—to even the most difficult situations merely by keeping their calm, remaining optimistic and feeling confident in their actions. Such an atmosphere keeps the "people problems" at bay and allows for freed-up time that leaders can use to pursue their passion.

Money isn't everything to a Pre-Emptive Leader but if he's following the system, it will be an inevitable outcome. Pre-Emptive Leaders attract success and earn every penny they make but, despite their achievements, tend to focus more on the needs and wants of others than on themselves.

Pre-Emptive Leaders sleep soundly at night because with their ability to live a well-rounded, ethical lifestyle, they are not plagued by worries or doubts. By making the right choices every day—and choosing, every day, to do the right thing—they create for themselves a mindset of confidence and optimism, and awake each day knowing that things will continue to go their way.

What's Next?

Pre-Emptive Leaders hold themselves to high standards when it comes to getting the job done—and getting it done *right*. In the next chapter, we'll show you how Pre-Emptive Leaders' task and people convictions are continually tested, and how a "no fear" mindset helps them overcome these obstacles.

PART III
HOW CAN I INFLUENCE OTHERS?

So far, we have described the process and methods of Pre-Emptive Leadership and shown you the benefits—the "What's in It for Me?"—it can bring to your career and your life. Now, let's take a look at what you need to do to personally sustain Pre-Emptive Leadership and use your leadership skills to influence the people around you.

CHAPTER THIRTEEN

Believe in Yourself First

One of the most admirable traits shared by most Pre-Emptive Leaders is the clarity of their convictions—and their ability to stay true to what they believe, no matter what.

> *One of the most admirable traits shared by most Pre-Emptive Leaders is the clarity of their convictions—and their ability to stay true to what they believe*

When we talk about convictions, we're referring to the Pre-Emptive Leader's high standards—his focus not just on getting the job done, but getting it done *right*. Above and beyond this, leaders also have high standards when it comes to how they treat other people: They will settle for nothing less than the blend of trust, support and teamwork that the Pre-Emptive culture demands.

Though Pre-Emptive Leaders are secure in their beliefs, there will be times when their high standards and methodologies are tested by others in the organization who have more power, different opinions or—unfortunately—lower and thus conflicting standards.

These frequent challenges would be enough to put any reactive manager on the defensive, but leaders know that feeling intimidated is not the way to go. Instead, they meet challenges head on, with a "no fear" attitude and confidence that the *right* way will win out in the end.

First, Believe in Yourself

How many times in your life have you caved in when someone has challenged your ideas or beliefs? It's human nature to feel intimidated when someone tells you that what you're doing is wrong, or to doubt your own thinking and second-guess your opinions.

But when you're operating under the Pre-Emptive Leadership System, such doubts become nonexistent. The level of self-examination it takes to be an effective leader practically guarantees it! Instead of questioning your own standards and actions, you find yourself asking questions such as:

- Why would anyone want to follow someone who is not confident in their convictions?

- If I do not believe in Pre-Emptive Leadership—and do not promote it as a standard of high quality within my organization—why would anyone else?

People need *something* to believe in—*someone* to believe in—and someone to believe *in them*. The Pre-Emptive Leader is more than ready to step into that role; all he has to do is have confidence in himself and persevere, no matter how rough the road ahead can look.

A leader does not get discouraged. He knows that anything worthwhile takes time to build and grow, and that he has the talent, skill and conviction to see any project through to completion, and do it by his own standards, not everybody else's.

What to Expect When You're Working With the System

As you put the system into place within your company, there are certain events and challenges that you can expect to face. In our many years of helping organizations implement Pre-Emptive Leadership, we have noticed some of the following phenomena as common to all leaders who are in the process of making the transition:

- Reversal to the management style you were using prior to Pre-Emptive Leadership—unconsciously falling back into old, ineffective habits.

- Feelings of disgust toward those who are not following the Pre-Emptive System within the organization—and a loss of focus because of your preoccupation with their mistakes.

- Critics within the company who do not understand the system—some people just can't see its benefits, and so talk unfavorably about what they do not understand.

- Frustration because implementation of the system is not turning out to be as easy as you'd expected—you know that anything worth doing takes work in the beginning, but it can be a difficult transition.

- Lack of support from people you thought would "have your back"—even though you had anticipated, or at least hoped for, enthusiasm from those around you.

These, however, are all just temporary roadblocks. And as we mentioned above, even good things can bring with them a certain amount of hard work that must be done. If you're coming up against any of these challenges, do not become discouraged or start to feel as though Pre-Emptive Leadership isn't for you. It *is* for you; it is for everyone who wants to make a difference in their workplace and in their life.

170 — It All Starts With YOU

Just stick with it, and in time you'll find yourself easily jumping over such hurdles—with the Pre-Emptive Leadership principles there to help you reach new heights.

Reversing Into Cruise Control

Let's go back for a moment and look at the first hurdle in that list we presented in the last section: the reversal to the leadership style you were using prior to Pre-Emptive Leadership. When you've been operating in a reactive environment for a long time, it's not unusual to feel some initial resistance to new ways of doing things. To counteract this, you need to be set on where you're headed and on the goals you hope to achieve by utilizing the Pre-Emptive Leadership System.

Also keep in mind that it's okay to retain some aspect of your previous management style. Take a minute now to look back at the way you used to do things, and see if there are parts of it you can leverage—and which aspects of it you might be able to smooth out, refine and work with in a whole new way. In our experience working with thousands of leaders, we have identified some such behaviors that are often on the "to be smoothed out" list:

1. **Jumping to conclusions.** This can be smoothed out by listening to others more intently instead of concentrating on your own thoughts and opinions.

2. **Telling others what to do.** This can be smoothed out by *communicating* and asking more questions rather than barking orders.

3. **Making all decisions by yourself.** This can be smoothed out by trusting others to make the best choices for themselves—or at least getting their input when you're deciding what to do.

4. **Letting frustration win.** This can be smoothed out by being patient, even when those around you are not doing exactly what you'd like them to.

5. **Holding on to a "my way or the highway" attitude.** This can be smoothed out by being flexible, letting others contribute their ideas and even letting those suggestions influence a decision's final outcome.

Identify two or three of your own specific behaviors that you can start smoothing out now to bring you closer to being the Pre-Emptive Leader you desire. Let the people around you know as well that you're working on these skills; remember that expressing a need for self-improvement is not a sign of weakness! Besides, you'll be amazed at the number of people you'll find to support you as you grow into the leader you want to be, simply by asking for their help.

When You Don't Get the Support You Need

Unfortunately, everyone around you may not be an enthusiastic supporter of the Pre-Emptive Leadership approach. These new methods you're using will be so innovative that some may need some convincing before they will give you their full backing.

Such a challenge can be disappointing, but not impossible to overcome. While trying to convince those nonbelievers that the Pre-Emptive System is really the best way to go, keep in mind the following barriers that reactive managers often face when confronted with major changes:

- **Management habits are hard to break.** When people have been settled in a reactive environment for a long time, they become firm in their opinions and staid in how they interact with or manage people. In short, they are stuck in their ways, and may not like how you are trying to influence them.

- **Apathy sets in.** Reactive managers may be content where they are and with the way they're doing things. They've carved out a comfortably numb existence for themselves and do not want to make waves. Averse to change, they avoid new ways of thinking—exactly what you're trying to achieve—because it just takes too much energy.

- **They don't see the value.** Set in their own ways and means, reactive managers don't connect at all with the principles of Pre-Emptive Leadership. The passion that drives the system is not something they can relate to and so they do not see any benefits they might gain from it.

As with all difficult tasks, however, just give this one some time and you will see results. Use your leadership influence and be the example of what you want to create within your organization. Once these reactive managers see your approach in action, the value will come through to them, and then they will want to be a part of what you are doing as well. Once they see that you are getting results, they will want to know how they can do it, too.

Even Experts Have to Practice

Great leaders make everything look easy. Like highly skilled athletes, they perform their tasks with grace and agility, leaving observers wondering just how they can do so much so effortlessly.

The secret here is simple: To become such a proficient leader that your hard work is all but invisible, you must practice, practice and then practice some more. Through repetition of the methods of the Pre-Emptive System, they will become second nature to you, leaving you the time and energy to develop and use even more new skills and talents.

Refuse to Lose Your Focus

It can be so easy to let yourself become distracted from your goals. With so much going on around you, who could blame you for becoming frustrated, misdirected and unfocused on the things you need to do?

At times like these, however, it is vitally important to refuse to lose your focus—in fact, hold on to it with everything you've got. It's counterproductive to let your eyes stray from your target.

Instead, be the driving force. Be the leader by example, showing everyone around you that even if it takes a while, your goals *can* and *will* be accomplished. Use the methods that you know will work; don't give in to the "unconscious incompetence" of other managers who don't even know that they could be doing things so much more effectively.

Rather than being frustrated by those who will not support you in your efforts, stay true to yourself, and stay on course. It takes discipline to stand firmly behind your convictions at all times, but as a Pre-Emptive Leader, self-discipline is not something that you will be lacking.

In a Nutshell

Pre-Emptive Leaders have high standards and strong convictions—but that doesn't mean they don't come up against their share of challenges. The key is to remain strong in times of conflict, believe in yourself and display a "no fear" attitude. Keep charging ahead toward your goals, no matter what. With Pre-Emptive Leadership behind you, you are unstoppable.

When implementing the Pre-Emptive Leadership System, there can be obstacles and setbacks, such as difficulty breaking old management habits and lack of support from those around you. View all of these as temporary roadblocks that will move right out of the way if you keep focused on your target and stand firm in your convictions as a leader.

Though your old way of managing was clearly not working, there might be aspects of it that you can mine and refine to use with your new Pre-Emptive outlook. Find those traits that you can adapt to your new leadership style and leverage them.

The more you practice the Pre-Emptive Leadership skill set, the more of an expert you will become. Don't let lack of support from your coworkers—or even your managers—get to you. Just keep your focus and be the driving force that your organization needs to bring it into a new, more successful era.

What's Next?

Convincing your demanding, intense, business-minded CEO that Pre-Emptive Leadership will be a benefit to your company may take a little finessing. In the next chapter, you will learn how to put your own ego aside and communicate your ideas about the system as a viable business tool—one that will catch your CEO's eye and make him or her see that, without it, the company will not maximize its competitive edge.

CHAPTER FOURTEEN
Putting Your Ego Aside

Pre-Emptive Leadership makes such good sense that you'd think everyone would be able to see its benefits and eagerly work to implement the system in their workplace.

Unfortunately, this is not always the case. These days, most companies are run by CEOs that can best be described as the "alpha" male or female of the organization—they are smart, not averse to taking risks, demanding, and have little patience for talking about people and their feelings. They're tough, and that's how they've gotten themselves—and their companies—to the positions they're in today.

The downside to this intense tenacity? These in-charge men and women often have trouble admitting they need to work on leadership development within their businesses. Moreover, when presented with Pre-Emptive Leadership as an option, they sometimes will not even consider it! If what they're doing ain't broke, they figure why try to fix it?

As a leader, then, your task is to convince your business-minded CEO that the system is a tool that his organization can't live without.

176   It All Starts With YOU

If you walk in and present it as something *you* want to do, chances are it will not fly. But if you can put your ego aside and let your CEO know that the system will help the company achieve and maintain a leading edge over the competition, then you're more likely to gain his attention—and convince him that giving Pre-Emptive Leadership a try is imperative to his company's success.

Getting Inside the Alpha

People who can be described as "alphas" within their professional environments are often rough around the edges; "brash," "bold" and "demanding" are just some of the words often used to describe them. They're not big on people skills and are more likely to bark an order at you than to solicit your opinion on the best course of action to follow—and then bark at you again when you don't jump to do just as they say quite fast enough for their liking.

However, most of them probably do not see themselves this way at all. The only things they see are the results that come from their actions—getting things done is the number-one priority on an alpha person's list—and the handsome rewards they're earning for the risks they take and the outcomes they produce. Everything in alpha-world is going great; an alpha rarely thinks that he has to change anything about his management style or methods.

If you work under an alpha-type CEO—or even just a manager who exhibits these qualities—you are probably familiar with phrases such as:

- "It's my way or the highway."
- "I don't need to adjust to people—they need to adjust to *me*."
- "If they don't want to work for me, I'll find someone who does."
- "No one else 'gets it' as quickly as I do."

These are the types of messages that alpha managers convey to those around them on a regular basis. Intentional or not, the only thing this gets across to their employees—as well as their colleagues—is that the alpha person has a very healthy ego, and thinks that he is probably better than just about everyone he comes into contact with.

Putting Your Ego Aside

177

But this type of person doesn't always have to get that message across verbally. Alpha men or women are masters of sarcasm, of rolling their eyes at ideas they disagree with, of using body language to tell everyone else quite clearly how little they are respected. Alphas are so wrapped up in their own egos that they are practically incapable of having a conversation that does not revolve around the words "I" and "me."

It's not uncommon to have several managers in a workplace who come across this way—and who continue to do so almost unchecked for the majority of their tenure with the company. The reason for this? Simple: They're so overbearing, most people fear talking to them, much less have the guts to tell them outright that they're being rude, egotistical and downright alienating to those who work for them.

So the alpha managers simply go on in the same way day after day, unaware of how they are being perceived and running over those they should be supporting, inspiring and encouraging. In the long run, this leads to a myriad of destructive employee behaviors, such as:

Feeling discouraged. With so much negativity in the air, it's no wonder that employees working under an alpha-type manager will give up on trying to do their best. Their efforts become only halfhearted, and the productivity of the division—and even the company—can take a turn for the worse as a result.

Reverting to individual agendas. When the people in charge are not fostering an all-for-one culture, team members are likely to feel as though they have to watch their own backs—no one is looking out for them, so they just have to look out for themselves. This focus on their own needs and wants, instead of those of the team, again affects productivity since there will be no team consensus about the way that things should be done.

Passing around the negativity. Bad feelings are like the flu in a workplace: Once one person brings the bug into the environment, it's a sure bet that ten other people will be down with the ailment by the end of the week. When managers are constantly using their influence to reinforce negative attitudes among their employees, they are keeping alive a vicious cycle of discontent that will be hard to break, even for the most talented leader.

Opposing recommendations. The fact of the matter is that an alpha manager is still a manager, and what she says still goes. However, when she treats her employees with disdain, they will return the favor and lose any respect they may have had for her authority. When this happens, they are likely to go against the manager's orders, questioning her strategies or techniques. This creates just one more rift in the ranks, one more wedge between those who are "in charge" and those who no longer feel like part of the team.

Building walls. Over time, all of these factors will create a long, high and practically unscalable wall between team members and the alpha manager—and even between team members themselves. These barriers could lead to a total breakdown of responsibilities and production, leaving the manager with quite a mess to explain to the alpha CEO.

Let Balance Be Your Key

We all want—and *need*—to feel good about our work, to feel pride in what we do. This is an aspect of our ego, the thing inside us that not only tells us how good we are but that craves approval, that wants to do a good job so that we can hear those notes of praise in the voices of those around us. There's nothing wrong with this; it's a natural human instinct to want others to like us and like what we do.

These alpha CEOs and managers we've been discussing, however, take that concept to an extreme that can be difficult to deal with when you're looking to begin implementing the Pre-Emptive Leadership System within your company. As they've operated solely in the reactive mode for probably their entire career, they seem to have no concept of balance, no idea about the importance of practicing the "bicycle analogy" that we've discussed in previous chapters.

Putting Your Ego Aside 179

Let's take a minute to look back and review that analogy now, so that we might see this one-sided egotistic behavior in a better light. In Chapter 1, we asked you to look at your department, or even your whole company, as a bicycle, with the front wheel based on people skills and the back wheel encompassing the procedures, policies and responsibilities that keep the business structured. Take one wheel away and the bike doesn't work, and that goes for the organization as well. For success, you simply need both sides of the equation to remain in balance.

When alpha-type managers are in charge, however, such a balance is difficult to achieve. Because of their egocentric ways, their attention to front wheel and back wheel issues is skewed; they pay little attention to the front wheel "people problems" and concentrate too much on the back wheel rules-and-regulations side of things. Remember, it's "my way or the highway," and if you can't manage to follow the codes of conduct that the alpha manager or CEO supports, then you know which option he will invite you to choose.

Don't get us wrong—ego is actually critical to back wheel operations within an organization. When it comes to clarifying expectations or enforcing safety, operations or procedures, those in charge need to be fair, firm and frank—in other words, straightforward and honest, two of the most prominent qualities that Pre-Emptive Leaders possess. Furthermore, leaders know that when they have to make tough decisions in these areas, they will be doing the right thing for their teams and their companies, because they are able use their egos in the right way—for the good of all, not just for themselves.

The problem, then, is that alpha managers are unaware of how to balance or adjust their ego to the appropriate level. When enacting or enforcing rules in the workplace, they do so in an authoritarian manner—not with an air of camaraderie and teamwork, but with the message of "what I say goes, because I say so." They do not convey to their employees the feeling that following standard practices benefits everyone. Instead, they coerce people into obeying guidelines that they may not agree with or even understand because that is just what employees are supposed to do. In the alpha person's world, things—and people—are unfortunately just that black and white.

The Alpha Challenge

When it comes time for you, as a Pre-Emptive Leader, to present your idea to your alpha CEOs and managers—let's say you want to convince

By recognizing that you do not have to "win" the argument to get what you want, you can focus more on the subject itself

them to implement the Pre-Emptive Leadership System itself—you may find yourself at a bit of a loss as far as how you should proceed. These people can be, as they say, tough nuts to crack, and approaching them with a proposal for making changes within the company can seem akin to jumping off a high cliff without a parachute.

Typically, there are two ways in which people approach those with alpha personalities: Either they storm in with a headstrong personality and try to win the manager or CEO over simply by force of will, or they cower down and take the humble approach, hesitantly presenting their ideas and saying things like, "I'll understand if you don't agree." Neither of these is very effective.

The Pre-Emptive Leader's method of approaching the alphas is intuitive and efficient. As a leader, you can influence these difficult higher-ups not by clashing with them over the details of the things you wish to do, but by removing the competitive aspect of it altogether. By recognizing that you do not have to "win" the argument to get what you want, you can focus more on the subject itself, and not on the alpha person's hesitation to accept it.

In essence, what we're saying is that winning your CEO and reactive managers over to the Pre-Emptive Leadership side is not a win/lose situation—nor is it win/win or lose/lose. Instead, it's a situation that requires adjustment and flexibility, mostly on your part. You must, if you want to achieve the results you desire, put your ego aside, choose your words in the language that the other person will understand, believe in what you are proposing and confidently stay true to your convictions.

What you want to do here is appeal to the alpha person's egocentric mindset—not with mere flattery, but through simple common

Putting Your Ego Aside 181

sense. You know that your company would run better under the Pre-Emptive Leadership approach, and you're sure that with it, the organization could really become more profitable, achieve higher levels of teamwork, attract talented employees and reach more satisfied customers. Far from just a personal interest that would benefit no one but yourself, you truly believe that the system can make the company—and everyone in it—better.

To convey this to your CEO and managers, you must take a thoughtful approach. You want to remind them of how successful their company already is, and appeal to their own desires to keep it that way. Make everything about the business, not about yourself, and you'll at least get the foot in the door that you need to get things started.

While educating such skeptics about the system, keep in mind the following:

You do not need to be the know-it-all. A typical alpha personality will listen to what others have to say—and then turn around and use those ideas as their own. Put aside your own ego, which likes to get credit for its own work, and accept that the best way to get the job done here is to let the CEO and managers take ownership of the Pre-Emptive Leadership System idea.

You do not need to react to alpha behaviors. They may say that what you're telling them is preposterous, or give you twenty different reasons why your idea—and the system itself—won't work. Don't shut down because of such comments; they are just STORMing, and you can politely and confidently continue on with your message, keeping the end result in mind. Giving in to what these people want—an argument, a chance to show you that they are right and you are wrong—will do nothing but derail your good intentions.

You do not need to change other people's minds or behaviors. Steer clear of trying to do this, simply because it is not possible. People will think and do what they want, regardless of the wishes or reactions of others. It's a fact of life and of human nature; people can only change themselves when and if they want to, and any attempts on your part to do it for them will be a waste of time.

When meeting with the alpha people in your organization to discuss what you've learned about Pre-Emptive Leadership, spend your time and effort on getting your points across and presenting your ideas in the most positive and intriguing light possible. You might not be able to influence their opinions right away, but if you play your cards right, you just might be able to get them *interested*—and that is certainly a good first step toward getting things done.

How It Works in the Real World

In order to convince their alpha CEOs and managers to move forward on any topic that requires doing something different, leaders need to approach the topic from an area of concern for all involved—not just for their own jobs, salaries and reputations. This will not be a difficult thing to do, for, as leaders, they are already attune to what's going on around them and to the needs and wants of the people they work for and with.

But even in the best Pre-Emptive Leader, there is an ego aspect that needs to be put aside during this time of attempted transition. Everyone has an ego and no matter how good-hearted you are, at some point your instinct to look out for yourself will come into play.

So how can you put your ego aside in order to get the job done? It's all about being aware, actively listening, and understanding. Pre-Emptive Leaders know that they can use their egos most effectively when they apply them to back wheel issues, when they are in "doer" mode, confident about their expertise and recommendations to get things done. At times like this, it pays for the leader to instead use their capacity to listen instead of tell, to propose and suggest their recommendations in order to influence those who need to be swayed.

This is a difficult thing to do, however, when communicating with ego-driven people such as your company's alpha people. In this situation, it's almost better to take your "ego hat" off entirely, and just go

Putting Your Ego Aside

with the flow of the conversation, letting the alphas lead the subject where it needs to go. By allowing them to feel in control of things like this, you will undoubtedly earn their interest, because they will feel as though they are part of the process—not just the person listening to you talk about it. Rather than competing with them, influence them by suggesting, listening and remaining calm in the face of their sure to surface ego-driven comments.

As a Pre-Emptive Leader, you have a keen understanding of people—of their quirks and behaviors, their wants and needs. It's an integral part of your leadership style, and a factor that sets you apart from the rest. Here, you can use that intuition to your advantage by keeping in mind that the alpha's ego trip is not anything personal against you; it's merely a manifestation of his personal need to compete and win. By putting your own ego—your own desire to be in the lead—to the side and refusing to play this game, you will feel free from the intensity that an alpha person can bring to the conversation. You will concentrate less on the delivery, which might be demeaning and discouraging, and more on the meaning of the messages that are being exchanged between you both.

In a Nutshell

We've all worked with alpha CEOs or managers—intense people who are often unaware of how they are perceived by others. Their ego-driven focus on their own performance can bring with it an impressive knack for getting results, but also a lack of balance in their approach to dealing with people. Concerned mainly with back wheel priorities and getting the job done, they do not seem to realize how far they could go if they simply adjusted to the front wheel and used their leadership skills instead of their management skills.

But that doesn't mean that alpha CEOs or managers cannot be swayed in a better direction. When approaching them about implementing the Pre-Emptive Leadership System in your workplace, it's best to work *with* them to achieve the results you want. They will most likely rail against your ideas and try to convince you that the changes you want to make are too time-consuming, but stick with it—they just need a little help in seeing the bigger picture and are testing to see how true you are to your convictions. Have patience, and just allow them to absorb your ideas until they adopt them as their own. Persistence is all it takes for you to accomplish what's best for the company.

What's Next?

Every Pre-Emptive Leader must have a set of core competencies to work with. Though each person's skills will vary, it's clear that there must be a demonstration of ability in each area. In the next chapter, we'll discuss what these disciplines are, which are most lacking in companies today and the commitment you must be willing to make to sustain them.

CHAPTER FIFTEEN

Leverage and Build New Habits

As we have discussed in previous chapters, self-examination and self-improvement are two key aspects of your ability to become and remain a Pre-Emptive Leader. You must look at your leadership behaviors, habits and traits and continuously improve upon them for the betterment of your team and your organization.

The Core Competencies

Within the Pre-Emptive Leadership System, there is a set of six professional qualities—we call them *core competencies*—which you must leverage in order to be an effective leader. These include:

1. **Direction and purpose**: Know what you stand for, your leadership vision and mission, and how you're going to accomplish them.
2. **Teamwork and collaboration**: Include those you work with in all that you can; implement their ideas and suggestions to enhance results.

It All Starts With YOU

3. **Trust and respect**: Have faith that your team members will do what they say they will, and never knowingly mislead them about anything that will directly affect them.
4. **Drive and motivation**: Possess a sense of urgency and discipline to get things done.
5. **Accountability and candor**: Take responsibility for yourself and your work, and let those around you know that you do so. When you make a mistake, own up, and let them know that as well.
6. **Technical expertise**: You must know the "nuts and bolts" of your workplace, and acquire the knowledge to be the expert and/or create a team of experts.

Each leader's skills in these areas will vary, and that is acceptable. Everyone has their own talents, their own strong and weak points, and part of being a good leader is knowing how to use what you're good at. Leaders must be well-rounded enough to have a working knowledge of each core competency but, as with anything else in life, they will have some that they are better at than others.

Over the years, through our work with thousands of leaders, we've found that there are *particular* competencies that are the most lacking in organizations that are not effectively utilizing the Pre-Emptive Leadership System. That is, across the board, there are three specific areas that employees feel are lacking in their day-to-day workplace experiences: direction and purpose; trust and respect; and accountability and candor.

Perhaps not coincidentally, these three competencies tend to hinge on and play off of each other. Accountability does not work if clear goals have not been established; trust and respect are not possible if people are not candid with one another. The challenge, as a Pre-Emptive Leader, is to

> *There are three specific areas that employees feel are lacking in their day-to-day workplace experiences: direction and purpose; trust and respect; and accountability and candor*

keep these interconnected qualities balanced so that they *can* work together.

As a leader, you have to go beyond the simple rhetoric that reactive managers can get stuck in when it comes to these core competencies and instead of just talking about them, really make them come to life. To do this, you must develop new habits of your own that will promote these underrepresented qualities, and use them to influence the people you work with.

Direction and Purpose

Employees these days are becoming less and less interested in long-term goals, overall visions and big mission statements. Instead, they are interested in the immediate: What are we trying to do different *today*? What are we trying to do better? How will what I'm doing right now impact the big picture?

That's about as far ahead as they look, and there's nothing wrong with that. These aren't new questions; they're probably the same ones that every working generation has asked itself when evaluating its meaning in the business world.

The difference now, though, is that with the rapid rate of change in today's culture, employees must feel that they are part of making a difference and impacting change in their daily priorities; in other words, they must feel the results of their actions *right now*. They want to have a sense that they're not just adding to that big picture, but that they're a part of it as well. If they don't feel like they're "in on" what's going on around them, their results will be nothing but frustration.

This model of direction and purpose happens when there is a crisis within the organization. At times like this, people rally together and work as a team to find a way to fix the problem; there is a sense of urgency that impels the team to act, and to implement their solutions as soon as possible.

This is a form of synergy, which we've discussed in previous chapters—it's a way in which people band together and share ideas for the benefit of the team as a whole. In times of crises, this phenomenon happens because:

188 It All Starts With YOU

Everybody gets together to hear about the situation. There is a feeling of needing to be informed, to know what everyone else knows. In uncertain times, it's always a comfort to know that the people around you are going through the same things that you are.

Short-range objectives are provided. The solutions the team comes up with must be accessible, "doable"—they must be immediate goals that people can get their hands on and achieve.

There is a sense of urgency. Everyone involved must feel the gravity of the situation and the need to get it resolved right away. If there is not an air of emergency among the group, the team members' attention may wander, and the crisis may not get the attention it deserves.

People are enlisted to help. Everyone likes to feel needed, and when you're trying to solve a problem, more hands often make for easier work. As with so many other areas of the Pre-Emptive Leadership System, here, when people feel as though they have a stake in the project, they are more likely to give their all to getting it done.

Upper management is accessible and involved. To ensure a successful outcome, those who are doing the hands-on work feel support from those who are "in charge." When employees see leaders getting in there and working on the problem just as hard as they are, they will feel better about the work they're doing, and more empowered to see it through to resolution.

When all of these components are present during a crisis situation, the result is a collective win: Not only does the problem get solved, but the employees feel better about themselves, their jobs and each other, and even about upper management. They have seen that through mutual support and teamwork, they can overcome any obstacle; "crisis moments" are good for showing people what they're made of—and what they're capable of when they're working at their best.

Pre-Emptive Leaders, then, are charged with keeping this synergy, this direction and purpose, alive on an ongoing basis. They can do so by taking a cue from the model we outlined above, which works in any situation, whether it's an emergency or not. There's no need to wait for a crisis to be a great leader; utilizing your leadership communication skills is something that should be done on a daily basis to *pre-empt* such situations from arising in the first place.

Breaking Old, Bad Habits

To achieve an acceptable level of direction and purpose, Pre-Emptive Leaders take the time to discipline themselves—to make sure that their own focus is set on where they need to go, and what they need to do to get there.

But before becoming a Pre-Emptive Leader, you were undoubtedly part of a management team that was not so disciplined, that did things a certain way and expected certain outcomes. Management teams are often stuck in their own habits, and are inflexible and unwilling to change the way they do things. Here are some common bad habits that management teams engage in:

Top management figures out the priorities of the present situation behind closed doors. This doesn't mean that they don't have a plan—it's just that they don't always invite key people to create the strategy with them. This, of course, works against the creation of any sort of supportive environment among the team members.

Managers communicate their vision to team members via a PowerPoint presentation. This may be informative, but it's too cut-and-dried. People need conversation, questions and answers, especially when trying to comprehend new information that they are supposed to act on. Being engaged in the vision—not just having it thrown at them—gives them a sense of ownership, and thus more motivation to see it through to completion.

Long-term objectives are generated and given out. That is, they are produced by the managers, not by the team, and speak only to what the managers think is best for everyone. Often, they miss the mark, leaving employees feeling talked down to and thus unwilling to give their all to the cause at hand.

Direction and purpose get lost in the mix. Middle managers and supervisors are responsible for passing direction and purpose on to their team members but, unfortunately, it doesn't always happen as it should. Sometimes, it never happens at all.

Managers do not engage their people in "Pre-Emptive huddles" on a regular basis. Believing that they don't have time for these interactive team meetings, managers often forego them, showing just how little they understand the value of this new habit.

Management teams tend to have "Old School" reactions to daily situations: They call management meetings, make decisions, and then go out and enforce their decisions in their own respective areas of the company. To do this, the managers often call upon their most trusted employees and give them the responsibility of "making things happen"—thus breaking the disbursement of communication that is needed in the organization. This disjointed, snip-it approach creates a communication flow throughout the organization that is very similar to a rumor mill: Everything is passed on by word of mouth, and no one knows what exactly is true.

But leaders don't let things like that happen. Instead, they use their new habits—including their Pre-Emptive huddles—to create the following interactions amongst their employees:

- Clarity of purpose
- A heightened sense of urgency
- Passion for getting things done
- Teamwork and support

Leverage and Build New Habits

Calling everyone together in a huddle for a brief stand-up meeting ensures that everyone is on the same page. This sense of unity, of teamwork, creates momentum for solving the problem or completing the project, and ignites people to get things done. A simple Pre-Emptive huddle could consist of discussions centering on topics such as:

- **What's on our mind right now**: Present the problem or project in straightforward terms, so that everyone understands what's going on.

- **The customers we're focusing in on**: Let the team know which clients are unhappy or which have requested special parameters for their shipments, for example.

- **Our top three priorities**: Outline succinctly the three most important areas of focus for this project.

- **How we see it rolling out**: Project a little into the future and let everyone know what they can expect to see at the end of it all.

- **Helping us make it happen**: Leaders don't give orders to their team members—they ask for their assistance, thus giving them a choice in the matter and a stake in the project's outcome.

The importance of the Pre-Emptive huddle cannot be overstated, nor can the imperative nature of establishing direction and purpose for your team. To do so, you may have to call upon your skill sets in other competency areas including teamwork (getting everyone involved), drive and motivation (motivating people to get things done) and accountability (actually getting things done). The Pre-Emptive direction and purpose core competency is vital to your leadership, and establishing it from the beginning will set the tone for how your team members react to you in the future.

Trust and Respect

Pre-Emptive Leaders don't just talk the talk; they show their team members that they trust them through their actions more than anything else. This habit is the complete opposite of Old School managers, who often say that they trust their employees but *do* nothing to give this impression. When it comes down to daily interactions, in fact, in all of our work so far, we've discovered that reactive managers are:

- **Making most of the decisions** instead of sharing the task with their teams. This lets their employees know that they do not care about their opinions, or trust them to make important choices for themselves, the team or the company.

- **Talking about trust** rather than actually having faith in people and letting them act autonomously. There's a big difference between rhetoric and action. Team members will pick up on a manager's insincerity when he talks to them about the importance of trust; they will be even further convinced of it when he fails to ever let them make decisions for themselves.

- **Propping people up** by doing things for them when they cannot fulfill their commitments. This is easier than having to hold people accountable for their poor choices, which could lead to discipline or even termination of employment. Then, the manager would be burdened with going through the hiring process all over again. As we said, it's just easier for the reactive manager to avoid all that by doing people's jobs for them.

Though they may sometimes try to give the appearance that they do, reactive managers do not actually trust their people to make decisions for themselves, and the employees know this. It creates a cycle of mistrust that prevents the development of teamwork and collaboration. It also keeps the team from being directed, and makes people unmotivated to succeed. Focusing on Pre-Emptive core competencies becomes impossible in a

Leverage and Build New Habits 193

situation like this because even if you try to be a leader, the self-perpetuating cycle will drag you back into reactive management mode.

The remedy, then, is to leverage your new Pre-Emptive habits. These include:

Allowing people to succeed or fail on their own. This habit is truly a hallmark of leadership; breaking free of the old management habits of mistrust and over-control is imperative to the Pre-Emptive competencies.

Getting employees' input. Team members need to know that you respect their expertise, that they are valuable to the team and that you need their thoughts and ideas. If you cannot muster any of these feelings toward your employees, then you might be hiring the wrong people or recruiting the wrong people for your team.

These two habits, it would seem, are so simple that they're almost unbelievable. Can leadership be as easy as letting people decide things for themselves and asking their opinion from time to time? The answer is: Yes, sometimes it can be. Other times, of course, it will be more difficult, but when you're honing in on the Pre-Emptive trust and respect competency, it really doesn't take much more than that.

Accountability and Candor

When an employee does something wrong—as any human being is bound to do at some point—generally, if it's not too egregious an offense, a simple discussion will remedy the situation: "This is what happened, let's come up with a plan for not doing it again in the future."

Seems easy enough, doesn't it? Well, it is—unless you're a reactive manager, many of whom really struggle with having tough, direct conversations with employees who have let them down. They dread having to talk about situations that have arisen due to an employee's shortcoming for fear that the person in question will be offended or

194   **It All Starts With YOU**

that a discussion will only make things worse. In the worst-case scenario, the reactive manager simply is not willing to take the time out of his or her day to work through the performance issue with the team member because there are just too many other things to do.

Other reactive management habits that show employees a lack of engagement include:

- Keeping thoughts to themselves.
- Avoiding situations that they perceive as confrontational.
- Adding the "performance issue" to the employee's personnel file rather than pre-empting the problem.
- Talking to other people about the team members they are frustrated with.
- Procrastinating when it comes to resolving the problem; leaving the conversation in "wait and see" mode.
- Taking action only when forced because the problem has become too big and they can't take it anymore.

Pre-Emptive Leaders, on the other hand, know that their new habit of practicing accountability and candor will pay them back in dividends, if they make the time to use it. This leadership skill goes beyond a means of dealing with errant employees; it works toward creating upfront, self-managed team members that in turn generate self-performing teams. This skill is an invaluable way for Pre-Emptive Leaders to duplicate themselves in the workplace in order to accomplish more than other managers.

The accountability and candor habit promotes trust and respect for the individual team member. To fully utilize this skill, leaders should:

Give employees honest feedback and direct updates on perceptions and expectations. Don't beat around the bush or try to gloss over the real problem. Trying not to hurt feelings doesn't benefit anyone in the end; being upfront about the problem—and collectively fixing it—is what brings the results that you're after.

Pursue conversations when you are disappointed in your employee's performance rather than walking away and venting about it to others. Ignoring the problem will not make it go away, and gossiping about it will surely compound it even further. As a leader, you must be above the rumor mill and Ahead of the Curve when it comes to being forthright with your employees—especially the difficult ones. They are the ones who need your help the most.

Be candid. It's the right thing to do because everyone needs to know where he or she stands. There should be no guessing on the part of team members when they feel like they might have made a mistake, and no form of discipline or reprimand should be sprung on them out of the blue.

Coach the individual. People deserve to know what the current perspective is so that they can develop their skills and be accountable for their work, or move on to something that better matches their personal values and objectives.

Summarize expectations or concerns to ensure that they are understood. After a one-on-one meeting to discuss performances or problems, the leader and the employee should "recap" what was discussed as well as any plans that have been agreed upon just to make sure they are on the same page as far as expectations and goals for the future.

Start with the employees you have now. Don't plan to be accountable and candid with whomever you hire next. Practice this competency with your current team members and they will notice a difference; your candor will be a refreshing change in their overall working environment.

Motivational Habits Versus Manipulation

Pre-Emptive Leaders develop habits to leverage motivation in their employees, nothing more and nothing less. The intent here is to help, not to harm—to earn the trust and respect of their team members, not to get them to bend to their leader's will.

The goal with these new habits is to turn them into skills, into permanent fixtures in your overall leadership character. In order for these new Pre-Emptive habits to become skills, though, you must be open to receiving help from those around you. Letting others know what you are working on will help you keep your commitments to these new habits; in other words, the public nature of the endeavor will ensure that you hold yourself accountable for achieving your long-term goals.

Reactive managers, as we've seen, are not interested in building new habits and this is probably because they are not concerned with developing their leadership style. They may talk about wanting self-improvement but, again, it's all rhetoric. Lacking the motivation to turn their words into action, they remain exactly where they are, with the same habits they've always had. Most goals that reactive managers have are inherently short-term in nature, and so the managers fail to see the value in working on something so over-arching and comprehensive that it could lead to a complete overhaul of the way they work—and the way that they influence other people.

As a Pre-Emptive Leader, you should never be trapped in such a box. You should have a thirst for continual learning, a desire to build new skills whenever possible. These are qualities that many leaders share. Other prominent characteristics of those who seek to create a strong leadership style include:

- **Focusing on doing the right thing.** While some of these new habits may feel awkward or harsh, Pre-Emptive Leaders keep the overall picture in mind and forge ahead.

- **Matching these new habits with meeting their career goals.** All three of the competencies we discussed in detail in this chapter will favorably affect relationships, opportunities for upward mobility, leadership skills and financial objectives.

Leverage and Build New Habits

- **Giving right now the investment of quality time.** A little effort upfront is all you need to get these new habits into your repertoire; once you've become used to them, you can go on to make them everyday skills within your leadership style, an automatic part of the way that you lead those around you.

- **Knowing your motives for implementing the new habits.** Maybe your motive is to stand out; maybe you want to be recognized or prove that you can become a great leader. Whatever your motivation, be clear about it—to yourself and others—in order to keep up your momentum.

- **Being honest.** It's as simple as that: Be honest with yourself and others about what you're doing and why you're doing it. As you work on your new habits, ask others for help and support to keep yourself accountable for attaining your goals.

- **Practicing by doing.** Nothing ever gets done just because we think about it; likewise, Pre-Emptive habits will not become part of your innate leadership style if you never put them to practical use. Don't wait until you feel perfectly comfortable; your ease is not supposed to be your first concern while you're trying to build new habits. Jump in, get your feet wet and try them out; the more you do, the easier it will be in the long run.

In a Nutshell

To be an effective leader, you must leverage the core competencies—particularly the ones that are usually most lacking in reactive managers: direction and purpose, trust and respect, and accountability and candor.

You can break any "Old School" management habits you may have by replacing them with more productive Pre-Emptive habits, such as holding team huddles, being upfront with your employees about expectations, problems and goals, and encouraging teamwork and

198　　　　　　**It All Starts With YOU**

motivation. If any team members are not fulfilling their expected roles, be honest with them about that as well. Candor in such situations can mean the difference between future success and ongoing, continued misbehavior.

Remember that teaching yourself new habits—and turning them into permanent leadership characteristics—is about helping the people you work with, not manipulating them. As a leader, you are always looking for cooperation and trust among your team members, not just to get them to do whatever you say.

What's Next?

Pre-Emptive Leadership is not about personal gain, but about assisting your team members to do their jobs well without resorting to demands or manipulation. In the next chapter, we will see how leaders' teaching and coaching skills—and their ability to balance them with the necessary managerial skills—can influence those around them and get results.

CHAPTER SIXTEEN
Teach, Not Preach

Think back to some of the great teachers you've had in your life. Maybe there was an exceptional teacher who encouraged you and helped you explore future career opportunities that would incorporate your talents; maybe you had a coach who not only taught you how to do a perfect lay-up, but also reminded you about the importance of getting good grades in addition to high scores.

Teachers often come in more nontraditional—that is, non-school—environments as well. Think about your parents, and all the lessons they may have taught you: to push yourself to succeed, to do the things you love, to believe that you can be or do anything that you set your mind to.

Pre-Emptive Leaders are also teachers, falling under this "nontraditional" category. Some people might not consider their leaders—the people who are in charge in their workplaces—as people to learn from. But with the Pre-Emptive Leadership System in place, each interaction between employee and leader is an educational opportunity.

Be the Teacher They Need You to Be

Although a Pre-Emptive Leader's job is, first and foremost, to keep the division or company running efficiently, productively and profitably, there

> *To influence their opinions, then, and to win their trust, you must act not as their manager or their boss, but as their teacher*

are also aspects of leadership that go above and beyond the everyday tasks and paperwork. Of course, you already know this—we've already shown at length how important it is to build trust with your employees, create good relationships with them and utilize those relationships to get the most out of your team members as far as productivity is concerned.

But you can't just walk into a leadership situation and expect everyone to be ready to jump right into the system. Employees who have been operating under a reactive manager for a long time may be resistant to the changes that you're eager to make because they are unfamiliar with them; they only know what they've experienced so far and, for all they know, "Pre-Emptive Leader" means the same as "same old manager we're used to."

To influence their opinions, then, and to win their trust, you must act not as their manager or their boss, but as their teacher. Instead of barking orders and handing out reprimands when expectations are not met, you must show your team members explicitly how they can take their assignments and get them done in the easiest and most productive ways possible. In short, you must inspire them (like that teacher who took an interest in you or the coach who believed in you) to take their skills and talents and use them to go above and beyond the levels they've been capable of in the past.

This can be a challenge. Humans are naturally resistant to change, especially when it comes to the people who are, in essence, telling them what to do. And if your team has been in reactive mode for some time, they will expect you to do things a certain way; they will look for you to make demands, manipulate situations in your favor and nag them constantly about deadlines or quotas, preventing them from doing their work efficiently.

Of course, they are in for a surprise.

When you take on the Pre-Emptive Leadership role, you are putting yourself in a position where you will be able to help others learn how to work to their full potential—and then help them put that talent into practice.

The First Step

Pre-Emptive Leaders love working with people—it's that plain and simple. Personal interaction on a professional level is what keeps leaders going, what inspires them to try harder in everything they do.

Of course, there are always exceptions. Even in the Pre-Emptive Leadership System, there are those who become more concerned with their own achievements than with the team that they lead. Too blinded by their own egos, they think that they are great leaders, capable of lifting the team to new heights that it could not possibly attain on its own.

This desire to achieve is admirable and probably good for the company's profits but, in the long run, it will not work. Even though people such as this claim to be leaders, it's clear to anyone who truly subscribes to the system that they are misclassifying themselves. There's a big difference between leading others to success—and teaching others to find success themselves.

Your job as a leader who teaches is the latter. You find satisfaction not only in teaching your team members how to do their jobs well but in mentoring them—in showing them how they can become more than they ever believed they could. You have a strong drive to invest in people not for the return it will give you but for the rewards it will bring the people themselves. Your passion is not just for results but for getting results through the people you work with in a way that benefits everyone involved.

Use Your Skills

You may be thinking that because you don't have any formal educational training under your belt, you don't qualify to teach anything to anyone. But instead of coming up with reasons why you can't, look instead to the Pre-Emptive Leadership model and the skills that you have gained because of it:

A knack for bringing out the best in people. As a leader, your interactions with employees are positive; even in the face of crisis, you stress the "upside" and motivate those around you to do the same. Your optimism and drive inspire others to work to their potential; a good teacher uses enthusiasm to bring life to any subject, no matter how difficult or disliked it might be.

Inspiring trust. Because they know that you will always "have their backs," your team members give you their full faith. Trust is an important component in learning—who will believe in a teacher who is untrustworthy? When it comes time for you to fill that role for your employees, you will have their attention as well as their dedication.

Working as part of the team. While teachers must have a certain air of authority, they should also give their pupils the sense that they are all in the learning process together, that they all have a stake in the sharing of information. Leaders utilize this same technique when they show their employees that they are willing to give them hands-on training, or to troubleshoot a problem with them instead of handing down orders and expecting them to be followed with no involvement on their part.

Being a good role model. The most effective way to teach people is by having *them* do the talking rather than *you*. Telling alone—what we like to call "preaching"—does not signify or create commitment. Your team will get more out of seeing you model the right way to handle situations than they will from hearing a speech about how to do it.

There are more similarities between leaders and teachers than you may think. All you have to do is use your leadership skills to be the teacher and coach that your team needs to lead it toward success.

Know the Difference

We said earlier that every interaction you have with employees is an opportunity to teach them something, and we do believe that's true. However, situations arise from time to time that call for you to rely on your back wheel skills—to be a manager for a few minutes instead of the leader that you are the rest of the time.

Deciding which "hat" to wear—leader/teacher or manager/doer—can sometimes be difficult, especially when it has to be done in a hurry, as is the case when you're working hands-on with your team members or when you first become aware that a crisis situation is developing.

To help you decide which way you should address a particular situation in the workplace—as a leader/teacher or a manager/doer—first decide what the underlying issue is. For example, if a team member comes to you with a concern about a coworker's contribution to the team, should you take it as a cue to coach him in the concepts of teamwork, accountability and confidentiality? Or, as his manager, should you tell him that he needs to focus on his own work and contribution? Which hat to wear depends on the situation.

As you lead your team, there will be many situations in which you will use your leading/teaching skills, and some that will require you to transition to your back wheel manager skills that ensure a culture of commitment. Some examples of each include:

- **Teaching Skills: Misunderstandings about the work that needs to be done**. If a particular employee is not operating to her full potential because the scope or procedures of a project have not been optimally communicated to her, take it in stride and recognize that you may have to put in some training time with her to bring her back up to speed. Don't simply give her the manual and let her figure it out herself, as a manager would do; take the time to explain the process or procedure again, knowing that your effort will help her produce better work in the end.

- **Managing Skills: Low productivity.** If, on the other hand, you have an employee whose production level is low and you've spoken to him about it already in the past, it's time for you to put on the manager's hat and let this person know that he really has to pick up the pace. You've probably already addressed the "people issue" surrounding the downturn in his output—that is, you've worked with him to understand the root of his issue and solve it in a manner that agrees with you both. If, after all your leadership efforts, it's still just not working out for him in the company, then you need to step up, be the manager and let him know.

- **Teaching Skills: Interpersonal issues.** If team members are in disagreement and come to you for mediation, coach them in conflict resolution and cooperation principles. If you can teach them how to develop solutions and commit to acting upon them together—without bringing you or another manager into it—then they will have the communication skills to resolve their own disagreements amicably in the future.

- **Managing Skills: Putting a plug on negativity.** As a leader, you strive to create a workplace environment in which no one *wants* to talk negatively about anyone else, but the fact of the matter is that it will happen anyway. When you become aware that the rumor mill has been put into motion or that malicious statements are being made, it's time for you to step in and use your managerial authority. To nip the behavior in the bud, remind your employees about the organization's core values and provide clear expectations.

It may seem as though leadership and management are two distinct entities that cannot exist in harmony with each other. But they can; it's just a matter of knowing which one to use at the appropriate time, and not letting one take over the other. As with so many things in life, running a successful business is all about balance, and being a

Teach, Not Preach

leader is about knowing when to be the mentor and coach your employees want and the manager that they need.

Teaching—and Keeping—the Best

When you successfully utilize your teaching skills with your team, you will see results. There will be improvements in morale, in trust and most importantly, in productivity.

To work to their fullest potential, sometimes your team members need a little coaching; they need a refresher on how to perform a task, or guidance on the best way to get things done efficiently. You can look at your team as a well-oiled machine: It works great most of the time, but there are always upgrades that can help it run even better.

And you are the one who is responsible for "installing" these upgrades. As the leader, you have to recognize when there is a need for education—for example, training, sharing information or discussing new ideas and methods—and then implement whatever is called for. For example:

- Have a new project with tasks that will be unfamiliar to your employees? Allot a day for training, even bringing in outside speakers or demonstrators if necessary to get them the information they need.

- Just hired a new employee who has great potential but rusty computer skills? Hook him up with the PC whiz in your division to get him up to speed.

- Noticing that morale seems a little bit low? Call a huddle— right now—and talk to your team members about it. Do some teambuilding exercises, or relate to them some pointers from an article you recently read about how to keep each other's spirits up when the work seems dull or difficult.

Education can take a thousand different forms; it's not always about saying, "This is how you do it," or "Let me show you a better way." It's about sharing knowledge and expertise, and utilizing the skills of your employees in conjunction to work more efficiently and be more productive.

If you can cultivate this sort of environment in your workplace—one in which your employees will see you as a mentor as well as a leader—then you are going to attract the best people to work for you. Good employees are a cornerstone of the Pre-Emptive Leadership System and the more you show that you are committed to helping your good employees become *great* team members, the more likely you are to bring in people who will be enthusiastic, intelligent and willing to work hard to make the business—and themselves—a success.

Of course, amongst all this greatness, there will be the occasional underperformer. Sometimes, employees think that they are up to the Pre-Emptive Leadership challenge—that they are ready to work hard, be a part of the team, follow the leader and be the best they can be—but when faced with these challenges in reality, they find that they are just not up to the task.

In cases like this, don't worry—you just keep on coaching and encouraging your team, and let these mismatched members work it out for themselves. More often than not, unhappy with the job that they're given to do, they will leave the company and seek employment with a competitor—where they can be comfortable in their old, reactive environment in which they are never challenged to go above and beyond.

The Payoff

Teaching your team members in any capacity is not an activity that produces results overnight. It takes time, effort and investment, and you may not see the fruits of your labor right away.

Coaching is a skill that requires patience—sometimes, lots of it. You might have to show someone a couple of times how to perform a task, or hold daily huddles on topics that are pertinent to your team's performance: better production methods, new motivational techniques, whatever they require to do their jobs better. You may even need to set up long-term teaching goals with periodic rewards along the way for team members who meet milestones and achieve the accomplishments and challenges that you set out before them.

An ongoing process such as employee education might be difficult for achievement-driven leaders to get a handle on. Part of being an effective leader is being constantly on the go—always on the floor, interacting with employees and being a part of the team yourself. When you're so used to focusing on what you need to do to keep everything running smoothly, on time and ahead of expectations, it can be difficult to take a step back and look at the big picture—which is exactly what your role as a teacher will have you doing.

But if you can work this role into your leadership repertoire, you will find that the benefits and rewards will be outstanding. All of the dedication and work that you put into assisting your employees to work to their full potential will pay off in time with greatly enhanced performance on the part of your team and, thus, greatly increased profits for your company.

If you're a great Pre-Emptive Leader—and we have no doubt that you are—then you will be a great teacher, coach and mentor as well. Just give it time, use your natural talents and let the rewards come to you.

In a Nutshell

A Pre-Emptive Leader's job is, of course, to lead—and with that comes an aspect of teaching, coaching and mentoring. Not just the person whom employees look to for instruction, a leader must also be a resource from which the team can gain guidance, education and training to help them do the best they can.

Coaching will come easily to Pre-Emptive Leaders, who genuinely enjoy working with people. Using their natural skill sets and talents—as well as those they have learned through the Pre-Emptive System—leaders can influence their employees to enhance their own skills and improve their own performance. This inspiration creates concrete results in the form of increased productivity and profits.

Keeping a balance between management and leadership is an important aspect of playing the teacher role. Leaders should always stay true to their people-focused methods and do whatever they can to help their employees become more than they think they can be. However, they must also know when to wear the "manager hat" and be the voice of authority that upholds company standards and practices. As with many things in life, effective leadership is about finding a balance between the two.

What's Next?

The old, reactive managers' mindset focuses on pushing productivity, and not on taking time to value the progress that got them there. In the next chapter, we'll look at ways in which leaders can promote repeated superior performance through celebrating achievements, offering incentives and keeping their own motivation in high gear.

CHAPTER SEVENTEEN

Celebrate Achievements

One of the main goals of Pre-Emptive Leadership is to increase productivity, which can be achieved through building solid relationships with your employees and fostering a culture based on trust and accountability. When these qualities are present in the workplace, people feel motivated to do their jobs well—and, in fact, to do even more than is required of them.

But when it comes to getting results, there is more to the equation than we see at first glance. It's true that if you invest in your team members by being their leader and not just their manager, the outcome will be increased productivity and greater profit for your company. However, you must also look at what else you can do to create consistent results—to reproduce these exceptional outcomes over and over, and keep the high productivity going long-term.

One of the best ways to do this is so simple that it often gets overlooked by reactive managers, who are apt to push their employees to produce, without stopping to appreciate the value of their increased efforts. Of course, that is an old mindset that is all but abandoned by Pre-Emptive Leaders, who know that one key to consistent results is taking the time to celebrate the win.

Celebration Myths

For people who have been stuck in a reactive environment for a long time, celebrating achievements—milestones in production, completion of goals, mastery of new methods and so on—will seem like an alien concept. But as any Pre-Emptive Leader knows, rewarding excellent performance is crucial to the progress of your division or organization. It's only by recognizing the employees' achievements that a leader encourages the team to keep up the good work.

However, there are some misconceptions about celebration—some celebration myths, if you will—that must be overcome in order to do it properly. To fully utilize this motivational tool, you must cast off the Old School way of thinking that still adheres to concepts such as:

Celebrating victories encourages people to slack off. Reactive managers believe that when employees are recognized for how well they're doing, they get too comfortable in their positions, overestimate their value and take it as a cue to start doing less. Pre-Emptive Leaders, on the other hand, know that rewards are excellent tools for encouraging continued achievements; it's human nature to crave recognition, and letting someone know that what they're doing is making a difference can really boost their desire to do even more.

Celebrations cost too much in time and effort. It's true—if you use company get-togethers or special team meetings as vehicles to recognize and reward exceptional employee behavior, then you might be losing some time that could otherwise be spent on production. But in the long run, those who work for you will remember that you thought enough of what they've done to take time out of the work day and devote it to honoring them—and that sort of special recognition will not be forgotten. In fact, it will be rewarded with increased effort and dedication.

Celebrate Achievements

211

Celebration is a phony gesture that does not make a difference in results. Because reactive managers tend not to invest in their employees, they do not recognize the powerful effect that celebration of great achievements can have on the workplace culture. They see rewards only as superficial actions, tokens that they have to hand out because they have been told to do so by their superiors. The Pre-Emptive Leadership System, on the other hand, encourages celebration and the value it brings to the team or company; instead of seeing the process as a chore that must be done, leaders celebrate achievements right along with their team members, knowing that rewards increase self-worth in the workplace, and thus increase productivity.

Employees should not need extra rewards for what they're already getting paid to do. This is true; even in the Pre-Emptive culture, we expect team members to work to their full potential because they believe in their work, their team and their organization—not because they think that they will be given a party or a trophy for doing well. But that doesn't mean that people don't need to feel valued from time to time. Celebration of achievements or milestones in a workplace that is already running efficiently and productively can be presented as an added bonus, something to be gained when the work is truly exceptional—thus encouraging not just *good* work but work that goes above and beyond the standard requirements. This overachievement is an expectation and a natural product of the Pre-Emptive Leadership culture.

Celebration ruins employees' focus. For a manager in a reactive environment, there is always the fear that any celebration—even if it's just taking a few minutes out of the workday to acknowledge performance—will interrupt the flow of production and throw everything off track. This reservation comes from a lack of belief in one's team members; if you really know who you're working with, you will know that they are accountable and trustworthy enough to be able to take a break, enjoy the celebration, and then go right back to what they'd been doing. This is the sort of dedication that Pre-Emptive Leaders inspire in their teams.

The Importance of Measurement

When considering how much leaders and their teams have to get done every day, one has to wonder how taking time out for celebrating can be rationalized. But it can be, and it must be. Celebration is not just an excuse to stop working for a while and hand out accolades for the sake of letting people hear their own names. This method of rewarding good work is a profound means of not simply recognizing employees but inspiring them and motivating them to go on to bigger and better things.

Consider, as a comparison, a workplace in which no one is rewarded for their achievements. Employees work hard day after day, meeting and often exceeding their goals but with no recognition for their dedication and skill. What motivation do they have to continue on in the same manner? If their manager gives them no clue either way—whether they are doing good work or bad—then what reason could they have for keeping up the same pace and level of quality?

The answer is simple and obvious: They have no reason to keep on overachieving. If they sense that no one cares how hard they work, team members will naturally feel less motivated to work to their potential. They may still fulfill requirements and occasionally rise above what is expected of them, but if they receive the same treatment whether they put in the extra effort or not, they cannot really be blamed for their lack of enthusiasm and accountability.

Pre-Emptive Leaders understand this conundrum, and so work hard to make sure that employees know how much they are valued. Leaders comprehend the importance of celebration of employee efforts, which shows team members that someone is actually watching what they're doing, and keeping track of their successes as well as their stumbling blocks. After all, part of achievement is the overcoming of obstacles, and it is often those who have overcome the most who have the best reason to celebrate.

Pre-Emptive Leaders intrinsically understand this need for measurement of employee performance. Whether they use charts and

Celebrate Achievements

figures or just keep notes in their heads, monitoring the progress of each team member is a vital part of leadership—as is helping each employee move ahead and achieve.

How to Say "Thanks!"

The eventual product of Pre-Emptive Leaders' continual observation of their employees is the celebration that we've been talking so much about. The more leaders see how hard their teams are working and how much the organization's productivity is increasing as a result, the more obvious it becomes that a reward of some sort is in order.

Thanking each individual in his or her own way can go a long way toward building and maintaining your foundation of trust

But what, many leaders wonder, is the appropriate celebratory offering? Handshakes? Free lunches? Monetary bonuses? It's difficult sometimes to tell exactly what the right reward would be in a given situation, and sometimes the accomplishment can be so exciting, it would seem like it's appropriate to go all out.

But grand gestures are not always necessary to let your team members know that you've noticed their good work. Sometimes, it is just a simple handshake and a "congratulations" that make all the difference. Not every employee needs to see their name in lights; a lot of attention can be embarrassing to some people, who would prefer a more private, personal acknowledgement.

As a leader, it's your responsibility to know your team members well enough to discern which of them want the simple approach, and which would appreciate a little more fanfare. Thanking each individual in his or her own way can go a long way toward building and maintaining your foundation of trust, and encouraging them to continue the high productivity for which they are being rewarded.

Motivating Yourself

Even though you're the leader, you still need your own rewards once in a while. You need the motivation to keep yourself performing at an optimal level on an ongoing basis, if for no other reason than to provide a good example for the people who work for you.

But if there is no one there to pat you on the back and tell you that you did a good job, how are you supposed to feel this sense of self-worth when it comes to your work? This often happens when a Pre-Emptive Leader is operating within an organization that is still mired in reactive management, or that hasn't quite yet fully made the switch to the Pre-Emptive System. Without people above you who recognize the achievements you have made as a leader, it can be difficult to gauge what kind of job you are doing.

What you must do, then, is judge for yourself, and give yourself your own pats on the back. Though this may seem a little more ego-driven than many leaders would be comfortable with, think of it more as a confidence-building act. There's nothing wrong with stepping back, looking objectively at the work you've done and recognizing, even if only to yourself, that you've met or even surpassed the goals that you've set out for yourself.

Giving yourself such accolades works in your favor by helping to keep your own motivation high. Pre-Emptive Leaders do not necessarily thrive on personal recognition, or on hearing other people tell them how well they did. They are more self-sufficient than that, and get more out of knowing that they achieved better results than they had expected to.

Leadership is an ongoing personal and professional challenge to oneself—to do more, be more and achieve more than you ever thought possible. Leadership is about being driven to work by the work itself, and about viewing the work as its own reward. It is this motivation that keeps you striving for excellence on an ongoing basis, and inspiring the people around you to do their best for the good of the company.

In a Nutshell

To keep employee motivation high, leaders must recognize and reward those who excel in their work. Doing so inspires team members to continue producing consistently high results over the long term—not

Celebrate Achievements

215

for the accolades, but for the innate good feeling that comes from achieving more than they thought would be possible.

While reactive managers look down upon celebrating team achievements as costly, phony and downright detrimental to employee productivity, Pre-Emptive Leaders recognize the value of celebration and utilize it as a tool to encourage even greater results.

> *It is up to you to keep your own motivation to succeed and excel*

Pre-Emptive Leaders also know that the reward must fit the employee. Not everyone will want to share their accomplishments with their coworkers; for some, private recognition is more motivating than public celebration. Know which style your employees prefer and cater to that when it comes time to recognize and reward, and your team members will reward you back with trust, hard work and continually increasing productivity.

It can be said that the leader sets the tone of the workplace culture, and so it is up to you to keep your own motivation to succeed and excel as high as possible. If there is no one available to recognize your achievements for you, celebrate them yourself, and feel the pride that comes from a job well done. Then, go out and use that as motivation to go even farther next time—and to motivate your employees to do the same.

What's Next?

At the heart of Pre-Emptive Leadership is the ability to walk the walk and not just talk the talk. To be a great leader and create a Pre-Emptive culture within your organization, you must have your heart in it; your enthusiasm, dedication and drive must be authentic, and really reflect the essence of true leadership. In the next and last chapter, we will discuss what it means to *be* a Pre-Emptive Leader, and how you can achieve the discipline you need to help you get there.

CHAPTER EIGHTEEN
Be a Pre-Emptive Leader

To be authentic is to be true, and it's clear by now that truth lies at the heart of the Pre-Emptive Leadership System. The culture that you create as a leader is based on a reciprocity of loyalty and truth between you and your employees, as well as on your own ability to be self-leading and true to your own character. It also relies upon a fine blend of give and take between you and those you lead.

People want leaders who are real, credible and, above all, believable

In any situation, followers respond to leaders who are true to themselves and to others, and this is one of the reasons Pre-Emptive Leaders are so successful: They know that in order to create the synergy that a thriving workplace requires, they must first look at their own behaviors and habits that might be keeping them from achieving all they can. Pre-Emptive Leaders are self-aware, self-reflective and willing to change whichever of their own traits are keeping the team from going further.

When team members see this dedication on the part of their leaders, they respond to it with loyalty, motivation and productivity. People want leaders who are real, credible and, above all, believable. Employees want leaders they can trust and rely on, and Pre-Emptive Leaders are able to give that reassurance to their team members over and over again.

Not All Leaders are Pre-Emptive

Changing over to the Pre-Emptive System requires work on the leader's part. There must be dedication to the principles of the system as well as a belief in what it stands for. There must be the willingness to self-examine and to adjust any personal habits that might prevent you from being an effective leader.

This is a lot to ask of one person—but there are, we've found, plenty of people who are up to the task. To many who seek to implement Pre-Emptive Leadership in their company, the techniques and standards of the system seem almost completely natural; often, they are ideas that the leaders have already had on their own, but might not have known how to pursue. Pre-Emptive Leadership is simply able to give them the push they need to get them going in the right direction.

Unfortunately, however, not all those who wish to be leaders will succeed. Many, many people are attracted to the Pre-Emptive Leadership System because of the core values it stands for: honesty, trust and accountability, just to name a few. These are, of course, highly desirable qualities; so many people want to be a part of the system as soon as they hear about it.

The truth, though, is that not everyone is ready for it. Some are not prepared for the sort of dedication that Pre-Emptive Leadership requires, the concentration they will have to put into it and the honesty that being a true leader entails. Perhaps these people can lead in a general sense of the word but, in reality, they simply do not possess all that it takes to become a Pre-Emptive Leader.

And what is it that they're missing? To start, it's a sensitivity to the needs, wants and ideas of others. Our research indicates that some people who wish to become Pre-Emptive Leaders just do not have a grasp on one of its most important aspects: the ability to understand where their employees are coming from, and to empathize with issues that they might have.

This lack of insight into the perspectives of others can be a real stumbling block for someone who wishes to be a leader—in fact, it has the potential to derail an entire career. Though they may wish to pursue Pre-Emptive Leadership as a means to gain employee trust and increase productivity, any progress that a leader could make in this situation would be false; if there is no *real* trust in the workplace, there will be no foundation on which to build a solid leader-employee relationship.

Change Is Possible

Fortunately for those who want to be Pre-Emptive Leaders, the lack of understanding described above is a personal trait that can be changed. Prospective leaders who do not possess the ability to understand their employees on a personal as well as a professional level do not have to be stuck in that mindset. It is possible, through self-discipline and concerted effort, to become more capable when it comes to dealing with people.

But again, this takes effort and a willingness to be honest with oneself. Not many of us like looking at our dark side and acknowledging that we need to change; we would all like to think that we're perfect just the way we are. But that's not realistic, of course, and so it's up to anyone who wants to be a true leader to dig deep inside themselves and muster up the courage to turn their *inability* into an *ability*. All they have to do is want it badly enough.

It takes a strong person to admit that they're wrong about something, especially when it's such a personal issue. But anyone who can do it—anyone who can transform themselves into true Pre-Emptive Leadership material—will show just how much character they have, and project the image of someone who is self-leading and ready to lead others. Followers respond to leaders who are true to themselves and others, and taking the steps to revamp your image in favor of Pre-Emptive Leadership is a good place to start.

Acquiring Discipline

Instilling yourself with the drive to want to become a Pre-Emptive Leader takes discipline—something that leaders have to begin with, but that can also be continually developed over time.

While working to acquire the discipline you will need to effectively implement Pre-Emptive Leadership, there are several things that you need to keep in mind:

There will always be naysayers and critics. Every good idea has its enemies, and that's no different where Pre-Emptive Leadership is concerned. You must learn to hear what they say, but not to listen to them; it's important to know what the "other side" is saying, but imperative that you don't let their words affect your overall outcome.

Leadership is not about being soft. Some people confuse the characteristics of a Pre-Emptive Leader with those of a "soft" manager—one who does not practice a good balance between valuing employees and holding them accountable for their own work. Being an authentic leader means having a backbone, especially in times of conflict, while still being understanding about the issues that your team members have. They will respect someone who can both listen to their problems and provide them with solutions. Employees want leaders with a healthy sense of who they are and what they want, not someone who will do whatever anyone asks just to please them.

Leadership starts with your own personal growth and development. We've said it before: To be a great leader, you must first look at your own habits and rectify whatever does not fall in line with the methods of Pre-Emptive Leadership. You cannot tell others what to do until you are doing it yourself. Besides, changing your ways to become a better leader really shows those around you that you mean business—and that you have the discipline it takes to lead them to success.

You are still a part of the organization. This all comes down to your ego: You must keep it in check no matter how good a leader you think you are. Presenting yourself as better or more effective than others will do nothing but set you back, and cause you to lose respect from those you work with. No one likes to be made to feel inferior, and you cannot be a Pre-Emptive Leader if you come across as more important than anyone else.

Taking risks will be necessary. When you are disciplined enough to be an effective leader, however, you will have no fear of unknown elements or outcomes. In fact, you will be willing to take risks when it comes to pursuing a Pre-Emptive course of action because you already know that it will have a high probability of success.

Pre-Emptive Leadership is a process. One of the greatest aspects of discipline is patience—the ability to delay our own gratification for the payoff of greater success in the long run. When implementing the Pre-Emptive Leadership System in your organization, this is how your results will come: incrementally, slowly, not all at once and certainly not right away. Results will occur in increments, and slow ones at that, but as a disciplined leader, you will feel a great satisfaction at the gradual but deep changes as you watch them unfold.

Balancing Everyone's Needs

As a Pre-Emptive Leader, you must walk a fine line between what is best for your team as individuals, and what the company as a whole wants or needs. On the one hand, you have the loyalty to your employees, and the innate sense that you must defend them and support them. On the other, you must also be accountable for things like meeting deadlines and fulfilling production expectations. In a sense, it's sort of a numbers push versus Pre-Emptive Leadership showdown. How on earth can you ever get these two to exist in peace, side by side?

> *It is possible, with Pre-Emptive Leadership, to balance the needs of individuals and the required demands of the organization*

It is possible, with Pre-Emptive Leadership, to balance the needs of individuals and the required demands of the organization. Again, this is something that takes a bit of discipline; as the leader, you must have the personal and professional strength to discern which priorities are highest and address each situation accordingly. For example, when a production deadline is looming, it's not the best time to call a meeting about a team member's lack of cooperation toward changing their work schedule; that is something that can be left for a later time, after the deadline is met.

When trying to form this balance between the two, keep in mind that it will not always be a perfectly stable situation. Often, one side will outweigh the other—organizational needs will trump employee issues, for example—but then later on, the scales will swing back the other way, and the latter will take priority. Don't get it in your head that you have to have both sides in perfect harmony from day one. As with so many other aspects of Pre-Emptive Leadership, this balance is on a give-and-take, case-by-case basis. All you need to do is have the wisdom—and the discipline—to know which situation needs to be addressed first.

Celebration Time!

If you've made it this far, chances are you're well on your way to becoming an authentic, heartfelt, trustworthy Pre-Emptive Leader, a person who is admired by employees, other leaders and CEOs. The work that you have done so far, the effort that you have put into implementing the system within your workplace, has already begun to produce results—including increased productivity, enhanced workplace satisfaction and your reputation as an example of reliability and accountability.

When you accepted the challenge of becoming a Pre-Emptive Leader, whether you realized it or not, you set yourself forth on a journey of self-discovery and professional learning. Being a part of the system has undoubtedly already benefited you personally by bringing out the best of your innate qualities—a desire for helping people, a need to do the right thing, the drive to achieve more with each passing day. Professionally, it has brought order to your workplace, meaning to the work you do and inspiration to those who are now proud to say that they work for you.

But the benefits of Pre-Emptive Leadership will not end here, with the closure of this book. This, in fact, is just a starting point—the springboard from which your greatest successes will launch. What you have begun to establish here will grow and flourish even further in the future, and will bring you returns that you'd never even dreamed of. Financially, professionally and personally, everything in your life is about to change. In fact, it's already started.

In a Nutshell

People respond to leaders who are true to themselves and to others, and so the air of authenticity that surrounds the Pre-Emptive Leader cannot be underestimated. By being self-aware and projecting an image of honesty and accountability, leaders reflect the essence of leadership—and win the loyalty, motivation and productivity of their team members in the process.

Though many people can lead, not everyone is a Pre-Emptive Leader. Often, it's a person's inability to grasp the needs of others that keeps him or her from performing at peak level and really embracing the Pre-Emptive System. However, as long as you possess drive, character and discipline to do so, you can develop this quality within yourself, and propel yourself forth to become a true Pre-Emptive Leader.

As a Pre-Emptive Leader, one of your biggest challenges will be striking the right balance between the opposing forces that will constantly be vying for your attention. Finding a way to satisfy your team members and the overall needs of the organization might be difficult at times but, as a leader, you will succeed—and do it with all the honesty and integrity that people have come to expect from you.

ABOUT XCELOGIC

Xcelogic helps organizations develop their leadership skills to deliver on core values, goals, and business strategies.

Pre-Emptive Leadership was developed by Mary Kay Whitaker and Ron Whitaker based on twenty-two years of testing, implementation and refinement. Today, the results of that effort can be seen across a wide range of industries with thousands of employees utilizing Pre-Emptive Leadership to become more effective, authentic leaders.

We have helped organizations such as The American Red Cross, BXWT Y-12 National Security Complex, The U.S. Department of Energy, National Nuclear Security Administration, Boeing, Mars Petcare, Shook Hardy Bacon, Koch Industries, Bosch, Leo A. Daly, Allied Signal, Gibbs Die Casting, Invensys, GBA, ANZA, Oil-Dri, Cardiovascular Consultants, *The San Francisco Chronicle*, Peterson Manufacturing and many others achieve an exceptionally productive team culture.

Pre-Emptive Leadership is a six-step system that does one thing extraordinarily well: develop human capital for breakthrough ROI. It addresses three of the biggest challenges facing organizations today:

Integrating Cultures

With M&A activity at a historically high level, more organizations than ever are facing a key question: How do you quickly integrate the best elements of varying workplace cultures?

226   It All Starts With YOU

How Pre-Emptive Leadership helps: Cultural issues *always* come down to providing direction, teamwork, expectations and communication alignment. Pre-Emptive Leadership establishes an easy-to-internalize method for integrating the best practices.

Creating a New Culture

Changing marketplace conditions, entry into new lines of business, transitioning to a new senior leadership team or other factors can mandate the need for an entirely new workplace culture.

How Pre-Emptive Leadership helps: Too often, attempts at organization-wide culture change come down to a reworked mission statement. Pre-Emptive Leadership gives *every* leader in the organization—from the C-suite to the shop floor—consistent tools for getting the best from people. *That's* the basis of long-term, high-ROI culture shift.

Developing Managers Into Leaders

Transformation requires leadership, vision and coaching throughout the organization—practices that task-based, reactionary managers often feel they have no time to undertake.

How Pre-Emptive Leadership helps: It delivers a proven process to communication. Your leaders spend *less* time repeating instructions, *less* time defining (and redefining) expectations…and *more* time helping the team excel.

> To learn more about how Xcelogic's Pre-Emptive Leadership System can work for your organization, please contact:
> Ron Whitaker (rwhitaker@xcelogic.com).
> www.xcelogic.com